wild
sweetness

wild
sweetness

RECIPES INSPIRED
BY NATURE

thalia ho

HARPER
DESIGN
An Imprint of HarperCollinsPublishers

To *You*, always

INTRODUCTION 11

—

BEFORE YOU BEGIN 12

INGREDIENTS 13

EQUIPMENT 15

EVERGREEN

page 20

amaretti
juniper and white chocolate ice cream
lemon curd streusel cake
fennel pollen pistachio cake
lemon thyme bars
cantucci
basil sugar pound cakes
herbs de provence loaf
lemon meringue cheesecake
basil chocolate sandwich cookies
after dinner mint pavé
dense fernet cake
crème de menthe ice cream
mint merveilleux

FLORA

page 52

petal granola
lavender scones
triple bean vanilla ice cream
elderflower sabayon
rhubarb and pink peppercorn tart
violet mousse
sea salt violet cupcakes
mendiants
frosted chamomile tea cake
white rose cake
rose walnut chocolate chip cookies
orange blossom crème caramel
chamomile shortbread
rose macaroon cake

BRAMBLE

page 88

ganache thumbprints
blackcurrant opera cake
almond paste cakes
chocolate cassis ice cream
blueberry almond scones
raspberry blondies
boysenberry frozen yogurt
clafoutis
currants and cream
frangipane tart
cocoa brownies
marquise
tayberry granita
strawberry sumac buckle

ORCHARD

page 122

late summer cake
pêche de vigne sorbet
plum and hazelnut financiers
red fruit crumble
dacquoise
dark chocolate cremeux
black forest cookies
fig clove fregolotta
mulled wine ice cream
drunken fig brownies
tart cherry semifreddo
bostock
oat biscuits with apricot, rosemary,
    and white chocolate
white peach and ginger cake

WOODLAND

page 156

truffles
beetroot mud cake
pecan scones
sugared sesame banana bread
malt and buckwheat ice cream
cinnamon buns
brown sugar cheesecake
buckwheat chocolate chunk cookies
rye bark
brutti ma buoni
double crumb halvah cake
bay leaf blondies
parsnip cake with tahini frosting
fallen chocolate cake

SMOKE

page 188

smoked fleur de sel brownies
tiramisu
walnut snowballs
burnt sugar ice cream
espresso marble cake
s'mores pie
rye chocolate sablés
black tahini brittle ice cream
bitter nib shortbread
scorched cheesecake
coffee parfait
molasses gingersnap cookies
teurgoule
winter citrus cake

BASICS

page 222

almond paste
brioche
chantilly crème
crème fraîche
streusel
crystallized nuts
frangipane
dreamy lemon curd
herbs de provence
pastry crust
rose ras el hanout
vanilla bean gray salt

INDEX   230

ACKNOWLEDGMENTS   237

"She was, finally, perfectly finished, perfectly heartbroken, perfectly wild."

—MARY OLIVER, *Devotions: The Selected Poems*

I HAVE AN ENDLESS LOVE for the wild. The greatest moments of my life have come from it. Of thorned, stolen brambles from the side of the road, and nights around the fire, smoldered and never the same. The afternoons spent under the old quince tree, the fruit, near rot; the scent, otherworldly. Those winters in the woods, swallowed whole. Each moment, precious, and rooted in earth.

To be free is what I have only ever demanded and I am free in nature. I'm at my best with feet in dirt and soil; a little primal, perhaps. It's been like this since childhood. I was raised with a strong connection to the earth, and if I think back, I see a girl within whom wild desire had been planted. I spent most of it outside, running toward something not even I'm sure of. Our home had a wood that bordered it then, and I remember the first time I lost myself. I couldn't have been more than five but I remember it well. It's where I shed my first skin.

There's something beautiful about impermanence, and the wild shows us that. It's fleeting. How rare to return to a place and it be unchanged, a season later. And while it isn't possible to experience the same moment twice, through food, it can be once again. A mouthful that tastes like a memory—brief, but never forgotten.

I never thought I would be here, in food. I wanted to become an artist. It's that pursuit that led me down many paths, oftentimes disorientated. The relationship between food and me has never been one of ease, for I was born with an insatiable hunger that left me starving. It almost ate me whole, but the wild is why I am alive. It's where I go to meet myself, and without it—I don't know where I would be. I owe a lot to it.

If anything, I know the strength that food has, the wild has, and at its core, that's what this is about. It seeks to sate a place far deeper than hunger, for both are more than fuel. Following a natural narrative is in our bones. Less about the external benefits of seasonal eating, and more about the internal ones, our own landscapes that need nourishing. And I believe in its strength, however devouring.

These chapters mirror the seasons, their essence, reflected. We begin early, in spring, with Evergreen, a herald of new life against the dark. The first of the flowers soon follow in Flora, a chapter that seems soft, but like a rose comes thorned. The heat hits in Bramble, a chapter bursting with berries and things to ease the swelter. And then, Orchard—it's a time of fleshed, fallen fruit, somewhere between late summer and autumn. It's teenage and the most transient, only lasting a few short weeks. A need for comfort arrives in Woodland, with warmth and spice, then finally, Smoke. It's intense and rich, wintered, and the one I delight in most.

A wildness exists within this book. It tells a tale of the natural world, and its influence, which bleeds into everything, even food. May it guide you to create your own tale, and become lost too. But please, let it be sweet.

BEFORE YOU BEGIN

This is a book written by a home baker for the home baker. It does, however, assume that you know your way around the kitchen. The following are things learned that helped me, and may just help you too.

INTUITION

I'm a firm believer in using your intuition. The kind that tells you to smell when a cake is done, to feel when dough has breath, and to sense the point between brown and burnt. I learned to cook from watching those around me, along with practice, reading, and refinement, over and over again. My intuition developed to where that knowing is a part of me, even if how I got it is elusive. If you can't feel it, you will. It might take some work, along with trust, time, and error, but we all have it in us.

INTENTION

I held on to a lot of what my grandmother taught me. Whenever she would work with dough, she'd set an intention. She'd tell me that it feels, as much as you or I, and it would never make good bread if there's even the slightest amount of tension in the air. It sounds flighty, but the more I cook, the more I see she's right. There have been many times when I've been stressed, anxious, pressured, or rushed, and whatever I'd been making suffered. So, before you start, come in with a good intention, and leave everything else behind.

MISTAKES

Mistakes will happen; let them. It's an important part of the process. Nothing is ever lost, only gained; if something isn't how it should be, now you'll learn and do better in the long run. Read, practice, and remember, you can always start again.

MISE EN PLACE

This translates to "everything in its place" and means that all items needed are laid out ahead so the process can run smoothly, without distraction or error. It's a useful practice, as the more organized you are, the easier it'll be, so set everything out in a clear manner that works best for you.

READ THE RECIPE

This goes without saying but it's a step often overlooked. Fall into the habit of reading a recipe, well, before you begin—start to finish, top to bottom, notes and all, then do it again and again until you feel it in your bones. If it tells you to do something a certain way, do it. There's a lot that's behind a recipe's construction, and even the slightest change could lead to something different. But don't let that daunt you. I've tried to leave enough guidance, but words only go so far. Again, read it through, use those instincts, and do a bit of research if you're still unclear.

INGREDIENTS

The following are found throughout these pages. Most are staples or ones that can easily be sourced. Others are a little more obscure, but useful.

alcohol: I like a stocked liquor cabinet. It's a trait learned from my grandfather, who has the most unique collection of bottles from all over the world—rarely for drinking but always for cooking. I use a bit of it in these recipes, but you don't need to have all the kinds included, as something similar will often substitute. I've made notes where possible to omit it too.

almond paste: Not to be confused with marzipan. I make it myself, as store-bought kinds are often too artificial in taste and don't contain enough nuts (page 223).

butter: These recipes use unsalted butter at room temperature, unless otherwise stated. It should be soft and malleable, but not to the point where it can no longer hold its form. I leave mine out on the counter for about an hour before I bake, but the time it takes will depend on the season, as well as the heat in your kitchen, so adjust accordingly.

chocolate: I like to use percentages when working with chocolate, rather than terms like bittersweet or semisweet, which vary in strength. Where dark chocolate is mentioned, it refers to a kind with around 54.5 to 70 percent cocoa solids. I don't call for milk chocolate or white chocolate often, but where I do, choose the best you can find, as their inherent sweetness needs complexity. A good rule is to choose a kind that you wouldn't just bake with, but that you would eat.

All cocoa powder must be Dutch processed and not natural, unsweetened, or Bourneville. The difference lies in their treatment. Dutch processed cocoa powder is alkalized, meaning that it's deeper, darker, and more mellow; better, I think, for baking. It's a bit sweeter too. Cacao nibs are also used. I consider them chocolate in its purest form, coming straight from the bean, with a bitterness that's great for offsetting sweetness.

coffee and espresso: These recipes use both coffee and espresso powder. I prefer a fine-ground kind over instant granules, which are often weaker in strength. I don't like store-bought versions either, so I use good locally roasted beans that I grind at home. Espresso powder is a more condensed form of coffee powder. I buy it online, as it's not often seen in stores. If you don't have it, use double the coffee powder instead.

dairy: All cream must be heavy or thickened and contain a milk-fat percentage of about 35 percent. Do not use reduced-fat alternatives. The same goes for milk, which must be whole or full-cream and not skim, low-fat, or dairy-free; all buttermilk should be cultured and pasteurized. I wouldn't switch the two out for each other, as it would likely throw off the acidic balance in a recipe. Milk should be at room temperature before use.

I like crème fraîche a lot. It's similar to sour cream, though more enigmatic, and the two can be used interchangeably (page 225). Mascarpone is a mild but rich cow's milk cheese. Its consistency varies, so choose one that's soft, creamy, and smooth. The same goes for ricotta. Cream cheese should be in block form and not whipped, spreadable, or light. I use plain or regular yogurt, as close to full-fat as possible.

eggs: These recipes were tested using large eggs that weigh about 2 ounces (60 g) each. I purchase free-range or farm-fresh eggs, not only for kinder practices, but also for their flavor and hue. Some recipes need either yolks or whites. I store leftover whites in the refrigerator for use within three days, or freeze them for up to three months. I find that yolks never keep well so I try to use them as soon as possible. Eggs should be at room temperature before use.

flour: Flour is all-purpose or plain and never self-rising, as it's easier to control the amount of leavening when it's added as a separate ingredient. I use alternate kinds a lot too, like buckwheat, rye, and spelt, which are great for strengthening baked goods. I don't recommend switching them out for regular flour and vice versa unless you're very comfortable with their ratios.

It's important to be accurate when measuring flour, and I will always recommend using a scale over cups,

but if you do choose cups, please use the scoop and sweep method. Whisk to aerate the flour, then scoop it into a heap and run a knife across the rim to level off the excess.

flowers: I use florals a lot. Though I prefer fresh, it's not always practical, and I purchase edible-safe dried flowers, like rose and lavender, storing them in the refrigerator to preserve their nature. I use essences and waters too. It's best to err on the side of caution when using these, as strength varies according to brand— so start small and work your way up, if needed.

While these recipes don't call for foraged or fresh flowers, I wanted to make a note that if at any time you do use them, as I sometimes will for decorating, they must be pesticide-free and edible-safe. Check with your florist before use.

fruit: These recipes use both frozen and fresh fruit; in season is best. I make a trip to the farmers' market each week, buying in bulk and freezing what I can't use right away.

herbs and spices: A well-stocked spice cupboard is a wonderful thing. Spices do, however, have a short shelf life and will become less potent with time, so I try to buy small and update as needed. It's important to store them correctly too. Seal tightly, in jars, and keep them out of sunlight.

Like spices, I use fresh and dried herbs to enhance taste. If a recipe calls for fresh, please don't switch it out for dried, and vice versa, unless it's rosemary, which can withstand the change.

leavenings: Non-aluminum baking powder and baking or bicarbonate of soda are used in a lot of these recipes. The two are not interchangeable. Baking soda needs acid to start it up, like lemon, buttermilk, or sour cream, and has a short shelf life. To see if it's still active, stir a teaspoon into a cup of warm water along with a splash of vinegar. If it fizzes, it's fine.

I also use instant dried yeast. It comes in small packets and doesn't need to be activated before use. I don't recommend substituting it with other forms of yeast, like fresh.

nuts, seeds, and grains: I buy nuts, seeds, and grains in bulk and keep them in big glass jars. I always have almonds, cashews, hazelnuts, pecans, pistachios, and walnuts on hand, along with a range of seeds too. All nuts should be unsalted, and sometimes roasted. To do this, preheat an oven to 350°F (180°C). Spread the nuts in an even layer on a baking sheet and roast for about 12 minutes, until golden brown. Cool before use.

oil: I use neutral oil, like canola, and sometimes extra-virgin olive oil in these recipes. I also use sesame oil. It's one of my favorite things to work with because of its smoky taste. Pick one that's toasted.

salt: Where salt is listed, it means iodized table salt. I keep many kinds of salts on hand for finishing too, like flakes, fleur de sel, gray salt, pink Himalayan salt, and black lava salt. You don't need them all; a couple that do it for you is enough. Most can be switched out for each other, but table salt is not a replacement.

sugar: This is a sweet book and there's a good amount of sugar in it. Granulated, or caster (superfine) is used most, as it's made up of fine crystals that dissolve well during baking. Raw sugar is large, coarse, and able to withstand heat. It's perfect for sanding or sprinkling. Confectioners' or icing sugar is a pulverized fine powder, and it should be sifted before use, as it can be quite clumpy. I also use light and dark brown sugar. While I always recommend sticking to what a recipe says, the two can often be switched out for similar results. I also use liquid sugars too, like honey, maple, and molasses.

tahini and halvah: Tahini is a smooth paste made from sesame seeds. It has a wonderful toasted taste and comes hulled or unhulled. These recipes were tested using hulled, which is creamier, a bit fattier, and less bitter. Make sure to give it a good stir before you use it too, as you would with peanut butter, to distribute the oils on top.

Halvah is a sweet Middle Eastern confection made of tahini and sugar. It's sold in blocks and comes

in a lot of flavors. I bake with plain or vanilla, but you could experiment with other kinds, like chocolate or pistachio. The options are endless.

vanilla: These recipes use pure vanilla extract, not imitation, essence, or any other synthetic—which pale in comparison. Vanilla bean pods are also used and should be purchased as plump as possible. It's fine to substitute one for a teaspoon of extract, though, preferably with seeds.

EQUIPMENT

It's important to use the right equipment. The items that follow are all listed throughout this book, some more than others. I've included notes on the ones I think are essential.

MEASURING

digital scale: An essential item for me. Though measurements are listed in both cups and grams, I recommend using a scale for accurate results, as the weight of a cup will differ each time. It's no secret that baking is a science, and just a few grams off could make all the difference.

measuring cups: If you do use cups, please check the system they're made for. These recipes were all tested for the US standard system, not metric, using metal cups in various sizes for measuring dry ingredients and a glass measuring cup with a pourable spout that's marked with increments for liquids.

measuring spoons: I rarely list things like spices, extracts, and salts that can be measured with spoons in weight, though I do for yeast, as it needs precision. I use a small set of metal spoons that range from ¼ teaspoon to a tablespoon, for measuring. Some will come with an ⅛ teaspoon attached, but I don't like it. It equals about the same as a pinch, and I prefer fingers instead.

TEMPERATURE

digital or candy thermometer: Nonessentials but good for peace of mind. I use a digital thermometer with a probe attached for an instant check on heat. It's useful for almost all recipes but not for deep-frying or candying, as it often won't read high enough. Most are made of plastic too, which isn't ideal when working with very high heat. A candy thermometer should be used in those situations. I use a stainless steel one with a clip attachment.

oven thermometer: An indispensable item. All ovens, gas, electric, and the like, are not created equal and will differ in their range of heat and dispersion. Mine runs hot, with a spot on the left that heats too fast, a spot on the right that's far too cool, and a good spot between the two. An oven thermometer is useful to prevent such inconsistencies from affecting baked goods. Choose one that reads Fahrenheit and Celsius and can be attached to a rack.

APPLIANCES

blender: Only a few of these recipes call for a blender. It's not something I use often, but a high-powered one is a useful piece of equipment to own.

coffee grinder: I use it to grind coffee, spices, and sometimes small amounts of nuts, like a mini food-chopper.

food processor: Something that I don't use often, but convenient when I do. It doesn't have to be a state-of-the-art machine, just one powerful enough to handle routine tasks like cutting butter, nuts, and biscuit dough.

ice cream machine: All of the ice cream recipes within this book call for an ice cream machine. I make a lot of it, and for me, it's an indispensable item. The machine I use has a built-in compressor with a pre-cool function, which means that the bowl does not need to be put in the freezer beforehand.

You don't need an overly high-tech, top-of-the-line one, though, and when I first started making ice cream, I didn't use one. I believe that the machine only accounts for a small percentage of the end result, and good ice cream comes from a well-constructed recipe, along with hands, eyes, and understanding.

stand mixer: A workhorse. While a good one can be expensive, it'll save you in the long run, especially if you bake a lot. I have two that I use

almost every time, as they let me focus on all the other parts that need attention while doing the bulk of the work. Most recipes call for a whisk, paddle, or hook attachment, but if you're without one, electric beaters, a wooden spoon, or whisk can act as a replacement in some situations.

SMALL TOOLS

biscuit cutter: Used for stamping out shortcakes, scones, biscuits, or doughnuts. I use stainless-steel round cutters that range from 1½ inches (4 cm) to 3 inches (8 cm) in diameter.

cookie scoop: Not an essential item but one that's more useful than you'd think. I use a scoop with a squeeze-release handle and a diameter of about 2 inches (5 cm) to portion out dough and small amounts of batter.

fine-mesh sieve: A versatile tool, used to sift and strain. Look for a metal, fine-mesh one, but not so fine that it resembles a tea strainer. It should have a sturdy handle and be able to withstand pressure.

kitchen torch: I torch rather than broil, as it allows for greater heat control. It's not an essential item, but one that's more useful than you'd think. It's good for unmolding chilled desserts like parfait too.

mixing bowls: I use glass and stainless-steel mixing bowls in a range of sizes for cooking and preparation. You don't need too many though. At least four, from extra small to large, will be enough.

rolling pin: A necessary item for rolling dough. A good pin can last a lifetime so choose one that feels good in your hands and care for it well. I use a wooden tapered-style pin that I bought in Paris.

small utensils: A wire whisk, wooden spoon, offset palette knife or spatula, slotted spoon, ladle, rubber spatula, ruler, knives, pastry brush, and pastry blender are all essential utensils used in this book.

wire rack: Choose a large stainless-steel rack that's grid-shaped, which will let air circulate well during the cooling process.

PANS, MOLDS, AND SHEETS

baking sheets: Sheets in various sizes are essentials. I almost always use two large, rimmed half-sheet pans that are 17 x 12 inches (43 x 31 cm) in size, along with a quarter-sheet pan and a jelly roll pan, on occasion. I like light-colored aluminum, but they don't have to be nonstick. I always line them, and a worn surface shows character.

cake pans: Most recipes call for round springform pans that are 8 inches (20 cm) or 9 inches (23 cm) in diameter. I also sometimes use an 8-inch (20-cm) square pan, which is great for brownies. I like to bake with various bundt tins

too, especially vintage ones, which range in shape, material, and size. If you don't have a similar one, something that can hold the same volume will be fine.

loaf pans: I prefer light-colored aluminum loaf pans over dark ones; I've found them to conduct heat better during baking. These recipes call for a standard-size pan with an internal dimension of 8 x 4 x 2½ inches (20 x 10 x 6 cm).

pie dishes: I always use a 9-inch (23-cm) rimmed glass plate for pies, as it distributes heat at a more even rate than ceramic or metal, and I love being able to see how the crust develops as it cooks.

specialty molds: Various molds are used throughout this book, for things like financiers and canelés. If you don't have the exact mold, use another close to the same shape and size.

tart pan: I like to use nonstick fluted tart pans with removable bases, for easy unmolding. I use a 9-inch (23-cm) round or 14 x 5-inch (33 x 13-cm) rectangular pan.

EVERGREEN

"Spring again, can I stand it shooting its needles into the earth, my head, both used to darkness."

– MARGARET ATWOOD, *Power Politics: Poems*

IT'S THE EVERGREEN that demonstrates there's life in darkness. Things are born from it. Winter comes to an end and suddenly, life shoots from the soil beneath. Nothing's ever dead. That's something nature doesn't tell but shows instead.

Like the earth, little by little, I pull myself together. For this is the season that tells me I cannot die anymore. I've always thought that the dark months are here to make sense of the light ones. For what is the spring worth if not the winter to give it purpose? There are moments when I refuse to let go, for it can be frightening to leave behind what kept you hidden and safe for so long. But the light is here to help.

The evergreen is a time of morning. First light, dawn chorus, and birds finding their voices. Of wind, gust, and thawing, slight chill on the skin, that no longer hurts too much. The first few weeks of it are never easy. After the long dark, things don't quite seem the same.

Your eyes have developed a way of seeing that light stings. Sometimes the adjustment is slow. Other times, a hemorrhage. There's no telling how it'll unfold. And that's beautiful.

It can feel like a remembrance. The earth sighs and wakes to itself, realizing what is, was once before. There's new life, a lot of it. Herbs, tendrils, and upshoots, through all things, growth. Sometimes, the last signs of winter will linger. Signified through dark, dense flavors and sometimes spice, but mostly it's bright. A lot lighter, cleaner, verdant, crisp, and tart in comparison with the comfort we've come to know in the cold months before. It can be a shock but, I do think, a welcome one.

I am going to do to my life what the spring does to the earth. I'll grow, be gentle and tender. I'll have strength, enough to look darkness in the eye and tell it, you never had me. I'll live wild and make it beautiful. And that'll be my life.

It has to be.

amaretti

makes about fifteen amaretti

I like the contrast of amaretti. Crisp, chewy, and crackled, yet soft, they're a textural explosion. Their flavor explodes too. I make them with honey and pistachio, along with lemon zest, which has a brightness that lifts the snow-stormed sugariness. They're a true embodiment of the season. Cold on the outside, but inside, life.

Combine the almonds, pistachios, granulated sugar, and zest in a large bowl.

In the bowl of a stand mixer fitted with the whisk attachment, whisk the egg whites until foamy. Meanwhile, put the honey in a small saucepan. Heat until it is at a bubble, then remove and pour it into the egg whites. Raise the speed to medium-high and continue to whisk for a few more minutes, until a shiny meringue has formed.

Add the dry ingredients to the meringue, and fold, to form a sticky dough. Cover with plastic wrap and transfer to the refrigerator to firm up a bit, about 30 minutes. Meanwhile, preheat the oven to 350°F (180°C). Line a large baking sheet with parchment paper. Put the confectioners' sugar into a shallow bowl for coating.

Using a teaspoon as a measure, scoop out generous, heaping, even-sized portions of the dough, then use your hands to roll each into a ball. If you have a scale, they should each weigh about 25 g. Coat in the confectioners' sugar, then set onto the prepared sheet, leaving a few inches of space between them.

Bake for 12 to 15 minutes, rotating the baking sheet halfway through, until crackled, puffed, and light golden brown. Let stand on the sheet for a few minutes, before transferring to a wire rack to cool until crisp. They'll keep for about a week stored in an airtight container at room temperature.

1 ⅔ CUPS + 1 TABLESPOON (165 G) GROUND ALMONDS

1 ½ CUPS (145 G) GROUND PISTACHIOS

½ CUP + 2 TABLESPOONS (125 G) GRANULATED SUGAR

ZEST OF A LEMON

2 LARGE EGG WHITES

1 TABLESPOON HONEY

½ CUP (60 G) CONFECTIONERS' SUGAR

juniper and white chocolate ice cream

serves four to six

Juniper has a sharp, piquant taste that's herbal, piney, and a bit citric. Whenever I use it, I like to pair it with something very sweet, like white chocolate, which has a cloy that offsets it. As we know, the cold blunts flavor, so it won't hit you on the nose, so to speak. Furtive, it's wonderful.

With a mortar and pestle or the side of a knife, crush up the juniper berries, then put them into a large saucepan, along with the cream and milk. Bring to a simmer then remove and set aside to steep for 30 minutes, giving it a stir every so often to prevent a skin from forming. Strain into a separate deep saucepan, pressing on the berries with the back of a spoon to release any infused juices, then discard them. Return to a simmer.

Meanwhile, whisk the yolks and sugar until pale and thick. Put the white chocolate into a large bowl, setting it aside but near the space where you'll be working.

Slip a little stream of the hot cream into the yolks, whisking constantly to acclimatize them to the heat, then pour it all back into the saucepan set on the stove. Continue to cook, stirring constantly, until it is thick enough to coat the back of a spoon. It shouldn't take more than a few minutes. Pour over the white chocolate and stir until melted. Cover with plastic wrap, pressing it onto the surface to prevent a skin from forming. Chill until cold, at least 8 hours, but preferably overnight.

When you're ready to churn, remove the custard from the refrigerator and give it a good stir to loosen, as it will have thickened up a bit. Transfer to an ice cream machine and churn according to the manufacturer's instructions. It'll be thick, creamy, and near doubled in volume when it's done. Scrape into a container, cover, and freeze until just firm before serving.

1 TABLESPOON DRIED JUNIPER BERRIES

2 CUPS (480 ML) HEAVY CREAM

1¼ CUPS (300 ML) WHOLE MILK

4 LARGE EGG YOLKS

¾ CUP (150 G) GRANULATED SUGAR

¾ CUP (130 G) FINELY CHOPPED WHITE CHOCOLATE

lemon curd streusel cake

makes an 8-inch (20-cm) square cake, which serves nine

This is all about lemon. It's bright, tart, and citric, because a good amount of curd seeps itself into the crumb. At times, I've been known to double the zest too, for something even stronger. It won't pucker, though, so if you aren't a fan of tartness, no need to worry.

Preheat the oven to 350°F (180°C). Grease and line an 8-inch (20 cm) square baking pan with parchment paper, leaving a slight overhang on the sides.

Whisk together the flour, almonds, baking powder, baking soda, and salt.

In the bowl of a stand mixer fitted with the paddle attachment, cream the butter and sugar on medium speed until pale and fluffy, 3 to 5 minutes. Pause mixing to scrape down the bottom and side of the bowl. Add in the eggs, one at a time, beating well to incorporate each addition, then beat in the vanilla and zest. Lower the mixer speed and tip in half the dry ingredients. Beat until just combined, then beat in the sour cream, followed by the rest of the dry ingredients.

Scrape the batter into the prepared pan, smoothing into an even layer, then stud over the curd. Scatter on the streusel.

Bake for 45 to 50 minutes, until golden brown. A skewer inserted into the middle should come out mostly clean. Let cool in the pan for 15 minutes, before transferring it out of the pan and onto a wire rack to cool further. Dust with confectioners' sugar, then slice into nine evenly sized pieces before serving.

1½ CUPS (190 G) ALL-PURPOSE FLOUR

⅔ CUP (65 G) GROUND ALMONDS

1 TEASPOON BAKING POWDER

½ TEASPOON BAKING SODA

½ TEASPOON SALT

⅔ CUP (1¼ STICKS + 1 TEASPOON; 150 G) UNSALTED BUTTER, *SOFTENED AT ROOM TEMPERATURE*

1 CUP + 2 TABLESPOONS (225 G) GRANULATED SUGAR

3 LARGE EGGS

1 TEASPOON VANILLA EXTRACT

ZEST OF A LEMON

¾ CUP + 2 TABLESPOONS (210 G) SOUR CREAM

½ CUP (100 G) DREAMY LEMON CURD (*SEE PAGE 227*)

STREUSEL (*SEE PAGE 226*)

CONFECTIONERS' SUGAR, *FOR FINISHING*

fennel pollen pistachio cake

makes a 9-inch (23-cm) cake, which serves eight to twelve

While fennel pollen comes from a flower, I see it as more of an herb than anything. It has a warm and vegetal flavor, with concentrated notes of citrus, honey, and anise. It's not too sweet, but it is strong, and a pinch goes a far way. A note on the glaze: I like it thin so the cake is partially revealed, like frost, but you can thicken it up too, adding in a bit more sugar until it's how you like it.

To make the cake, preheat the oven to 350°F (180°C). Grease and line a 9-inch (23-cm) round cake pan with parchment paper.

Whisk together the flour, ground pistachios, baking powder, pollen, and salt.

In the bowl of a stand mixer fitted with the paddle attachment, cream the butter and granulated sugar on medium speed until fluffy, 3 to 5 minutes. Pause mixing to scrape down the bottom and side of the bowl. Add in the eggs, one at a time, beating well to incorporate each addition, then beat in the lemon zest and juice. Beat in half the dry ingredients, followed by the milk, then the rest of the dry ingredients until light and aerated. Scrape into the prepared pan.

Bake for 45 to 50 minutes, until golden brown. A skewer inserted into the middle should come out near clean. Let cool in the pan for 15 minutes, before transferring it out onto a wire rack to cool completely before glazing.

To make the glaze, whisk together the confectioners' sugar and lemon juice until smooth. Pour over the cake, drizzling it so it runs down the sides, then decorate with the chopped pistachios and allow to set. It is best eaten on the day of making but can be stored in an airtight container at room temperature for up to 3 days.

FOR THE CAKE

OIL OR BUTTER, *FOR GREASING THE PAN*

1½ CUPS (190 G) ALL-PURPOSE FLOUR

1 CUP + 1½ TABLESPOONS (105 G) GROUND PISTACHIOS

1 TEASPOON BAKING POWDER

1 TEASPOON DRIED FENNEL POLLEN

½ TEASPOON SALT

¾ CUP (1½ STICKS; 170 G) UNSALTED BUTTER, *SOFTENED AT ROOM TEMPERATURE*

1 CUP (200 G) GRANULATED SUGAR

3 LARGE EGGS

ZEST OF A LEMON

2 TABLESPOONS LEMON JUICE

⅓ CUP (80 ML) WHOLE MILK

FOR THE GLAZE

1 CUP (120 G) CONFECTIONERS' SUGAR

2 TABLESPOONS LEMON JUICE

FINELY CHOPPED PISTACHIOS, *FOR FINISHING*

lemon thyme bars

makes eight bars

Thyme is herbaceous. It's aromatic, warm, and medicinal, but with a slight softness too. It's wonderful with lemon, as both share some characteristics, with others opposing, and it's this balance that makes these so wonderful. Use fresh thyme, not dried, or if you can find it, lemon thyme.

Preheat the oven to 350°F (180°C). Grease and line an 8-inch (20-cm) square baking pan with parchment paper, leaving a slight overhang on the sides.

To make the crust, whisk the flour, confectioners' sugar, thyme, and salt in a medium bowl. Add the butter and toss to coat, then use your fingers to rub it in to form large clumps. Tip into the prepared pan, pressing it into an even layer. Bake for 20 minutes, until light golden brown, then remove and set aside. Lower the temperature to 300°F (150°C).

Meanwhile, make the filling. Stir the granulated sugar and flour together in a large bowl, then whisk in the eggs and lemon juice, until combined. Pour the mixture over the crust. Return to the oven and bake until just set, 20 or so more minutes. Transfer to a wire rack and allow to cool in the pan, before lifting out and slicing into eight bars. Dust with confectioners' sugar. They'll keep for about 3 days stored in an airtight container in the refrigerator.

FOR THE CRUST

⅔ CUP (1¼ STICKS + 1 TEASPOON; 150 G) UNSALTED BUTTER, *SOFTENED AT ROOM TEMPERATURE*

1¼ CUPS + 1 TEASPOON (160 G) ALL-PURPOSE FLOUR

⅔ CUP (80 G) CONFECTIONERS' SUGAR

1 TEASPOON FRESH THYME LEAVES

¼ TEASPOON SALT

FOR THE FILLING

1½ CUPS (300 G) GRANULATED SUGAR

⅓ CUP + 1 TABLESPOON (50 G) ALL-PURPOSE FLOUR

4 LARGE EGGS

⅔ CUP (160 ML) LEMON JUICE

CONFECTIONERS' SUGAR, *FOR THE TOP*

cantucci

makes about forty cantucci

These come from Florence. There wasn't a night on that trip that didn't end with something sweet, often cantucci. Crumbly, buttery, and short, is how I remember them; misshapen too, and these are the kind I like best. They're filled with nuts, chocolate, ginger, and herbs, and are sweet but a little spicy. They're best eaten once they've had time to cool and crisp, but if you happen to get to them while they're still warm, the chocolate—molten and near set—is a bonus.

Whisk together the flour, thyme, baking powder, and salt.

In the bowl of a stand mixer fitted with the paddle attachment, cream the butter and sugar on medium speed until pale and fluffy, 3 to 5 minutes. Pause mixing to scrape down the bottom and side of the bowl. Add the eggs, one at a time, beating well to incorporate each addition, then beat in the almond extract and lemon zest. Lower the mixer speed and tip in the dry ingredients. Beat, until a soft dough has just begun to form, about 10 seconds. You don't want it to be well combined, but a bit shaggy, with a few floured pockets throughout. Beat in the almonds, chocolate, and ginger, until distributed.

Tip the dough out and onto a sheet of plastic wrap, and divide it into four portions, shaping each into a log. They don't have to be perfect. Cover and chill until firm, about an hour. Meanwhile, preheat the oven to 350°F (180°C). Line a large baking sheet with parchment paper.

Transfer a dough log onto a lightly floured work surface. Use your hands to shape it until it's about 1 inch (2.5 cm) wide, flouring as needed to prevent it from sticking. Transfer to the prepared sheet and brush with egg wash. Repeat with the remaining dough.

Bake for about 20 minutes, until light golden. Remove and let cool for a few minutes, then use a sharp serrated knife to slice each log into 1-inch-(2.5-cm) thick pieces, setting them back on the sheet, cut sides facing down, as you go. Return to the oven. Bake for about another 15 minutes, turning over the cantucci halfway through, until deep golden brown. Transfer to a wire rack to cool completely before serving. They'll keep for about two weeks stored in an airtight container at room temperature.

3 CUPS (375 G) ALL-PURPOSE FLOUR, *PLUS MORE FOR THE WORK SURFACE*

1 TEASPOON THYME LEAVES

½ TEASPOON BAKING POWDER

A PINCH OF SALT

½ CUP + 1 TABLESPOON (1 STICK + 1 TABLESPOON; 130 G) UNSALTED BUTTER, *SOFTENED AT ROOM TEMPERATURE*

1 CUP + 2 TABLESPOONS (225 G) GRANULATED SUGAR

3 LARGE EGGS

½ TEASPOON ALMOND EXTRACT

ZEST OF A LEMON

1 CUP (140 G) CHOPPED ROASTED ALMONDS

⅔ CUP (115 G) CHOPPED WHITE CHOCOLATE

⅓ CUP (55 G) CHOPPED CRYSTALLIZED GINGER

1 LARGE EGG, LIGHTLY BEATEN, *FOR EGG WASH*

basil sugar pound cakes

makes three 5 x 3-inch (14 x 8-cm) loaves, which serve eight to ten

The point of these is the sugar; the cake is nothing but a vehicle to transport it, albeit a good one. With notes of grass, the basil relieves the richness and enlivens instead. The recipe will make more sugar than you'll need and the excess can be sealed and stored in the refrigerator for use within the week. It's lovely paired with lots of things, even fruit.

Preheat the oven to 350°F (180°C). Grease and line three 5 x 3-inch (14 x 8-cm) loaf pans with parchment paper, leaving a slight overhang over the sides of the pans.

To make the cakes, sift together the flour, baking powder, and salt.

In the bowl of a stand mixer fitted with the paddle attachment, cream the butter and 1¼ cups sugar on medium speed until fluffy, 3 to 5 minutes. Pause mixing to scrape down the bottom and side of the bowl. Add the eggs, one at a time, beating well to incorporate each addition, then beat in the vanilla and zest. Beat in half the dry ingredients, followed by the buttermilk, then the rest of the dry ingredients until well combined. Divide among the prepared pans, smoothing out the tops.

Bake for 25 to 30 minutes, until golden brown. A skewer inserted into the middle of the loaves should come out clean. Let cool in the pans for 15 minutes, before turning out and onto a wire rack to cool completely.

Next, make the basil sugar. Put the ½ cup sugar, basil, and lemon zest in a small food processor or grinder. Process until even and fine, stopping before the mixture turns into damp clumps. It shouldn't take more than 20 seconds. Sprinkle over the cakes before serving. Store the excess sugar, covered, in the refrigerator for up to a week.

FOR THE CAKES

¾ CUP (1½ STICKS; 170 G) UNSALTED BUTTER, *SOFTENED AT ROOM TEMPERATURE, PLUS EXTRA FOR GREASING THE PAN*

1½ CUPS (190 G) ALL-PURPOSE FLOUR

¾ TEASPOON BAKING POWDER

¼ TEASPOON SALT

1¼ CUPS (250 G) GRANULATED SUGAR

3 LARGE EGGS

1 TEASPOON VANILLA EXTRACT

ZEST OF A LEMON

⅓ CUP + 1½ TABLESPOONS (100 ML) BUTTERMILK

FOR THE BASIL SUGAR

½ CUP (100 G) GRANULATED SUGAR

¼ CUP (10 G) PACKED FRESH BASIL LEAVES

ZEST OF ½ LEMON

herbes de provence loaf

makes an 8 x 4-inch (21 x 11-cm) loaf, which serves eight to ten

There's so much to say about this cake, that I don't think I can. It leads a double life. On the surface, plain; and beneath, anything but. It has a taste that can't easily be defined—sweet, but savory, herbaceous, fragrant, and warm. Nostalgic, in a way too. It reminds me of my grandmother. It seems an odd choice of words to describe it, but try it and you'll know what I mean.

Preheat the oven to 350°F (180°C). Grease and line an 8 x 4 x 3-inch (21 x 11 x 7-cm) loaf pan with parchment paper, leaving a slight overhang on the sides.

Whisk together the flour, almonds, herbes de Provence, baking powder, and salt.

In the bowl of a stand mixer fitted with the paddle attachment, cream the butter and granulated sugar on medium speed until fluffy, 3 to 5 minutes. Pause mixing to scrape down the bottom and side of the bowl. Add in the eggs, one at a time, beating well to incorporate each addition, then beat in the lemon zest. Beat in half the dry ingredients, followed by the buttermilk, then the rest of the dry ingredients, until well combined. Scrape into the prepared pan.

Bake for 50 to 55 minutes, until golden brown. A skewer inserted into the middle should come out clean. Let cool in the pan for 15 minutes, before turning it out and onto a wire rack to cool completely. Dust with confectioners' sugar before serving.

¾ CUP (1½ STICKS; 170 G) UNSALTED BUTTER, *SOFTENED AT ROOM TEMPERATURE, PLUS EXTRA FOR GREASING THE PAN*

1¼ CUPS + 1 TEASPOON (160 G) ALL-PURPOSE FLOUR

1 CUP + 2 TEASPOONS (100 G) GROUND ALMONDS

1 TABLESPOON HERBES DE PROVENCE (*SEE PAGE 228*)

½ TEASPOON BAKING POWDER

¼ TEASPOON SALT

1¼ CUPS (250 G) GRANULATED SUGAR

3 LARGE EGGS

ZEST OF A LEMON

½ CUP (120 ML) BUTTERMILK

CONFECTIONERS' SUGAR, *FOR FINISHING*

lemon meringue cheesecake

makes a 9-inch (23-cm) cake, which serves eight to twelve

The issue that I have with most cheesecakes is that they're too rich. Between the crust, filling, and sometimes topping, it can all be a bit much. This one is my ideal. It's light, luscious, and not too sweet, with most of the sweetness coming from the meringue top. I use a torch to singe it but you could use a broiler instead. Just keep your eye on it. You don't want the heat to reach the cake below.

Position a rack in the middle of the oven. Preheat to 350°F (180°C). Grease and line a 9-inch (23-cm) round springform cake pan with parchment paper, covering the outside with a few layers of aluminum foil. Bring a kettle of water to a boil.

To make the crust, put the graham cracker crumbs and almonds in a medium-size bowl. Stir in the melted butter until the mixture is evenly moistened. Tip the mixture into the prepared pan, using the back of a spoon to press it into an even layer. Bake for 10 to 12 minutes, until golden brown. Set aside to cool.

Lower the oven temperature to 250°F (120°C). Pour the boiling water into a deep roasting pan until it's about halfway full, then set it on the bottom rack of the oven.

Next, make the filling. In the bowl of a stand mixer fitted with the paddle attachment, beat the cream cheese until smooth and malleable, then add the sugar and beat until fluffy, 3 minutes. Pause mixing to scrape down the bottom and side of the bowl. Add the yolks, one at a time, and beating well

FOR THE CRUST

3 TABLESPOONS UNSALTED BUTTER, *MELTED, PLUS EXTRA FOR GREASING THE PAN*

⅔ CUP + 1 TEASPOON (90 G) GRAHAM CRACKER CRUMBS

¼ CUP (25 G) GROUND ALMONDS

FOR THE FILLING

2 (8 OUNCE | 450 G) PACKAGES CREAM CHEESE, *AT ROOM TEMPERATURE*

½ CUP + 2 TABLESPOONS (125 G) GRANULATED SUGAR

6 LARGE EGG YOLKS

½ CUP (120 ML) LEMON JUICE

1 CUP (240 ML) HEAVY CREAM

FOR THE MERINGUE

2 LARGE EGG WHITES

¾ CUP + 2 TABLESPOONS (175 G) GRANULATED SUGAR

ZEST OF A LEMON

to incorporate each addition, until well combined. Lower the speed. Beat in the lemon juice, followed by the cream, until thin and glossy. Strain into the prepared pan, using an offset palette knife to ease it through the sieve and smooth any lumps.

Bake for $1\frac{1}{4}$ to $1\frac{1}{2}$ hours, until just set. It should still have a wiggle to it. Turn off the oven and remove the roasting pan. Allow the cheesecake to remain inside with the door ajar, until it reaches room temperature, about another hour. Transfer to the refrigerator to chill until cold, at least 6 hours, but preferably overnight.

Just before you're ready to serve, make the meringue. Put the egg whites and sugar in the bowl of a stand mixer. Set the bowl over a saucepan filled with a few inches of barely simmering water. Do not let the base of the bowl touch the water below. Heat, whisking often, until the mixture reaches 160°F (71°C) on a candy thermometer. The sugar should be dissolved and the mixture hot to the touch. Set the bowl onto the stand mixer fitted with the whisk attachment. Whisk on high speed until thick and glossy, about 5 minutes, then whisk in the lemon zest.

Use the back of a spoon to swirl the meringue over the cake. Singe with a blowtorch, carefully, before serving. It will keep well, covered in the refrigerator for about 3 days.

basil chocolate sandwich cookies

makes about fifteen cookies

It seems strange, but basil and chocolate are a natural combination, like chocolate and mint. They like each other a lot. The sweet, fresh, and verdant notes find comfort in the bitter dark, resurrecting it, almost. It's subtle, and if you weren't looking for it, you'd be hard put to find it. I think that's how it should be, though: quiet.

To make the cookies, whisk together the flour, cocoa, and salt.

In the bowl of a stand mixer fitted with the paddle attachment, beat the butter and granulated sugar on medium speed until creamy, 3 minutes. Pause mixing to scrape down the bottom and side of the bowl, then beat in the egg. Set the speed to low and tip in the dry ingredients. Beat until a soft dough has just begun to come together, no more than 10 seconds. Scrape onto a sheet of plastic wrap, then halve, cover, and chill until firm, at least half an hour. Meanwhile, preheat the oven to 325°F (160°C). Line a large baking sheet with parchment paper.

Set half of the dough onto a surface dusted well with cocoa. With a rolling pin, roll it out until it's about ¼ inch (6 mm) thick, then stamp out as many circles from it as possible, using a 1½-inch (4-cm) cutter. Place them on the baking sheet, leaving a few inches of space between them, then reroll the scraps and repeat. It's a soft dough, so handle with care, dusting it with cocoa to prevent sticking and using an offset palette knife to help lift the cookies onto the sheet, as needed. Repeat with the remaining dough. You should have 30 cookies.

Bake for 8 to 10 minutes, rotating the pan halfway through, until firm to the touch. Remove and let cool on the sheet for a few minutes, before transferring to a wire rack to cool completely.

To make the buttercream, beat the butter and confectioners' sugar until smooth. Add the cream, vanilla, basil, and salt, and beat for a few more minutes, until light, fluffy, and aerated.

Turn half the cookies over. Pipe or spread a generous teaspoon or so of the buttercream onto them, then top with a matching half, using a light amount of pressure to sandwich it down. Set in the refrigerator to firm up, then serve, soon after. They'll keep for about 3 days, cold.

FOR THE COOKIES

1 ½ CUPS (190 G) ALL-PURPOSE FLOUR

½ CUP + 1 TABLESPOON (55 G) DUTCH PROCESSED COCOA POWDER, *PLUS EXTRA FOR DUSTING*

¼ TEASPOON SALT

¾ CUP (1 ½ STICKS; 170 G) UNSALTED BUTTER, *AT ROOM TEMPERATURE*

¾ CUP (150 G) GRANULATED SUGAR

1 LARGE EGG

FOR THE BUTTERCREAM

½ CUP (1 STICK; 115 G) UNSALTED BUTTER, *AT ROOM TEMPERATURE*

2 CUPS (240 G) CONFECTIONERS' SUGAR

2 TABLESPOONS HEAVY CREAM

1 TEASPOON VANILLA EXTRACT

2 TABLESPOONS CHOPPED FRESH BASIL

A PINCH OF SALT

after dinner mint pavé

makes about thirty-six pavés

When chocolate and oil meet, they cause a eutectic reaction, creating
a compound that melts or sets at a lower temperature than the original
ingredient. It sounds trivial, but it's important, as it makes things taste
softer, silkier, and richer. You'll notice it in these pavés, which have the
most mouthwatering texture, best served, I think, at the end of a meal.
They do melt fast, though, so get to them quick.

Grease and line an 8-inch (20-cm) square baking pan with parchment paper,
leaving a slight overhang on the sides.

Put the chocolate in a medium-size heatproof bowl set over a saucepan
filled with a few inches of barely simmering water. Do not allow the base
of the bowl to touch the water below. Heat over medium-low, stirring
often, until melted. Remove and stir in the coconut oil and peppermint.
Pour into the prepared pan, then transfer to the refrigerator to chill until
set, at least 4 hours.

When you're ready to coat, put enough confectioners' sugar into a shallow
bowl. Remove the chocolate from the pan, using the excess parchment
to lift it out and onto a cutting board. Cut into evenly sized squares. You
should get about 36 out of it, but how large or small you want them is
entirely up to you.

Working one by one, toss each square in the sugar until coated, then
set it aside onto a serving plate. You'll want to move quickly, as they're fast
melters. I like to use a knife to push them around, to avoid the heat from
my hands, and transfer into the freezer to firm up a bit if I notice them
becoming too soft. Keep cold until serving.

2 CUPS (340 G) FINELY CHOPPED
DARK CHOCOLATE

⅓ CUP + 2 TABLESPOONS
(100 ML) COCONUT OIL, *PLUS
EXTRA FOR GREASING THE PAN*

A FEW DROPS PEPPERMINT OIL

CONFECTIONERS' SUGAR,
FOR COATING

dense fernet cake

makes an 8 x 4-inch (21 x 11-cm) loaf, which serves eight to ten

Fernet is a digestif made from a range of herbs and spices, such as rhubarb, cardamom, myrrh, ginseng, and saffron. It's bitter, medicinal, and strong, and it's great to bake with too, as it does well with other things of strength, like chocolate. I use it to drench this cake, which makes the cake even more dense. If you can't find it, use another herbal liqueur instead.

To make the cake, preheat the oven to 350°F (180°C). Grease and line an 8 x 4 x 3-inch (21 x 11 x 7-cm) loaf pan with parchment paper, leaving a slight overhang on the long sides.

In a large mixing bowl, whisk together the flour, cocoa, baking soda, baking powder, and salt. Stir in the sugar. Push the dry ingredients around the side of the bowl to form a well, then whisk in the egg and crème fraîche, followed by the melted butter, until smooth. Whisk in the water, slowly. Pour the batter into the prepared pan.

Bake for 35 to 40 minutes. A skewer inserted into the middle should not come out clean but with a few, dense crumbs attached to it. The top should be split too. Set onto a wire rack.

Meanwhile, make the syrup. Put the fernet and sugar in a small saucepan. Bring to a simmer over medium-low heat, stirring often to dissolve the sugar, then remove and brush the syrup over the cake. Allow to cool completely before lifting it out of the pan and serving. It will sink into itself a bit as it cools.

FOR THE CAKE

1 CUP + 3 TABLESPOONS (150 G) ALL-PURPOSE FLOUR

¾ CUP (75 G) DUTCH PROCESSED COCOA POWDER

1¼ TEASPOONS BAKING SODA

¾ TEASPOON BAKING POWDER

½ TEASPOON SALT

1½ CUPS (300 G) GRANULATED SUGAR

1 LARGE EGG

⅔ CUP (160 G) CRÈME FRAÎCHE *(SEE PAGE 225)*

½ CUP (1 STICK; 115 G) UNSALTED BUTTER, *MELTED, PLUS EXTRA FOR GREASING THE PAN*

⅔ CUP (160 ML) HOT WATER

FOR THE SYRUP

¼ CUP (60 ML) FERNET

¼ CUP (50 G) GRANULATED SUGAR

crème de menthe ice cream

serves four to six

I will always return to mint chocolate chip ice cream. It's something that's entrenched within my bones, and I don't think I would be the same without it. This one isn't lurid, as many often are, but pale instead, relying on leaves and liqueur for its color. When you add the melted chocolate, be sure to stream it in slowly. The slower the stream, the more delicate the chip, which, I think, is the mark of good ice cream. Stop often too, so it can splinter.

Put the cream, milk, and mint leaves in a large saucepan set over medium-low heat. Bring to a simmer, then remove, and set aside to steep for 30 minutes, giving it a stir every so often to prevent a skin from forming. Strain into a separate deep saucepan, using the back of a spoon to press on the leaves to release any juices, then discard them. Return to a simmer.

Meanwhile, whisk the egg yolks and sugar until pale and thick in a medium-size heatproof bowl.

Slip a little stream of the hot cream into the yolks, whisking constantly to acclimatize them to the heat, then pour the mixture all into the saucepan set on the stove. Continue to cook, stirring constantly, until the mixture is thick enough to coat the back of a spoon. It shouldn't take more than a few minutes. Remove and stir in the crème de menthe. Strain into a bowl, then cover with plastic wrap, pressing it onto the surface to prevent a skin from forming. Chill until cold, at least 8 hours, but preferably overnight.

Just before you're ready to churn, melt the chocolate down in a small heatproof bowl set over a saucepan filled with a few inches of barely simmering water. Do not allow the base of the bowl to touch the water. Remove and stir in the oil. Set aside until needed.

Transfer the cream and egg mixture to an ice cream machine and churn according to the manufacturer's instructions. As soon as it's fluffy, thick, and can hold its shape, stream in the melted chocolate, slowly. Continue to churn until it is thick, doubled, and the chocolate hardened. Scrape into a container, cover, and freeze until just firm before serving.

2 CUPS (480 ML) HEAVY CREAM

1¼ CUPS (300 ML) WHOLE MILK

1 CUP (40 G) PACKED MINT LEAVES

5 LARGE EGG YOLKS

¾ CUP (150 G) GRANULATED SUGAR

2 TABLESPOONS CRÈME DE MENTHE

⅔ CUP (115 G) FINELY CHOPPED DARK CHOCOLATE

1 TABLESPOON VEGETABLE OIL

mint merveilleux

makes eight pieces

The name of these means "wonderful," and it's true, they are. They're composed of two chewy meringues that are slathered with cream, sandwiched together, then rolled in chocolate. Heavenly, to say the least. I ate a fair few when I was in Lyon, and I've haven't let it go since. This is how I remember them but also how I want them to be: dark, intense, and decadent, wintered but fresh.

Preheat the oven to 250°F (120°C). Line a large baking sheet with parchment paper.

To make the meringues, mix the confectioners' sugar and granulated sugar together in a small bowl. In the bowl of a stand mixer fitted with the whisk attachment, whisk the egg whites and salt until foamy. Add in the sugar mixture, a little at a time, until it is all used up, then raise the speed to high. Whisk until stiff and glossy. Pipe or spoon the meringue into 16 small 2-inch (5-cm) rounds on the prepared sheet, aiming to get them as even and level as possible.

Bake for 40 to 45 minutes, until light brown, then turn off the heat and prop open the oven door. Allow the meringues to cool inside until crisp, before assembling.

When you're ready to assemble, put the chocolate shavings into a shallow dish. To make the filling, put the cream, crème fraîche, confectioners' sugar, and crème de menthe in the bowl of a stand mixer fitted with the whisk attachment. Whisk on medium speed, to firm peaks.

Place a generous dollop of cream on top of a meringue, then sandwich with another, using light pressure to press it down. Cover with cream, smoothing it on with an offset palette knife. Transfer into the chocolate shavings, patting them on, until coated. There's no neat way to go about doing this, so do your best, and lick the excess. Transfer to the refrigerator to firm up for at least half an hour, before serving. They're best eaten the day of making, as they'll soften with time.

FOR THE MERINGUES

½ CUP (60 G) CONFECTIONERS' SUGAR

⅓ CUP (70 G) GRANULATED SUGAR

2 LARGE EGG WHITES

A PINCH OF SALT

2 CUPS (340 G) FINELY SHAVED DARK CHOCOLATE

FOR THE FILLING

1¼ CUPS (300 ML) HEAVY CREAM

⅓ CUP (80 G) CRÈME FRAÎCHE (*SEE PAGE 225*)

¼ CUP (30 G) CONFECTIONERS' SUGAR

1 TABLESPOON CRÈME DE MENTHE

FLORA

"I take refuge in roses, in words."

—CLARICE LISPECTOR, *A Breath of Life*

THERE ARE THINGS we can learn from flowers. How beautiful it is to bloom and flourish, then wither, returning to the soil to grow once more. It's work, but they do it and show us how to do it too. For it takes strength to flower, and even more to bear it. I know that well. The meaning of my name is to blossom, and if there's anything that it's taught me, it's that blossoming can hurt.

It's flowers that signify the spring. Violet, lilac, and rose, then later, lavender; their presence is a herald. I was born in the spring, which perhaps explains why it's the season I'm most connected to. There's a tenderness that comes with it, that permeates all I do. Just as I change, so too does my cooking. It's lighter, softer, and flushed—gentle, but at the same time, more potent.

I don't believe flowers are as fragile as we think. Known to pests, storms, and wandering hands, they know what it means to endure. Powerful, provocative, and dangerous in strength sometimes too. On the surface, delicate, but within, anything but. I remember the first time I tasted rosewater. I was very young, and took a swig, losing my senses for days. It was then that I understood why roses come thorned.

There's no need to fear their use, though. When incorporated with care, florals can be subtle and balanced, nuanced, with an entire world of other flavors residing within them, waiting to be released. A far cry from the overwhelm they've often come to be associated with. A rose is never just a rose, but a floral with hints of strawberry, peach, citrus, and musk—almond too.

I breathe in.

petal granola

serves about four

This is based on a Heidi Swanson recipe that I've always loved. I make it at the start of each week, switching it up on whim. A handful here and there, it's adaptable, but the one thing that always remains the same is rose. It has a delicate, feminine, and ethereal tone that I can't get enough of, softening the rough granola. I make it with honey and butter but you could use maple syrup and coconut oil for a vegan version, which is just as good, but less clustered.

Preheat the oven to 300°F (150°C). Line a large baking sheet with parchment paper.

Combine the oats, nuts, nibs, poppy seeds, and salt in a large mixing bowl.

Put the butter in a medium-size saucepan set over medium-low heat. Heat, stirring often, until melted, then remove and whisk in the honey and rosewater. Pour over the oat mixture, stirring with a wooden spoon until moistened. Tip onto the prepared sheet, spreading it into an even layer.

Bake for about 30 minutes, removing to stir every 10 minutes or so, until golden brown. Be sure to watch it carefully, as it will darken fast. Remove and immediately use the back of a spatula to press it into a flat layer, for clusters. Skip this step if you're making a vegan version, as the maple syrup won't bind in the same manner. Allow to cool before tossing with the fruit and petals.

Transfer to an airtight container and store in a cool, dark spot. It will keep for about a week.

3¾ CUPS (300 G) ROLLED OATS

¾ CUP (85 G) CHOPPED PECANS, HAZELNUTS, ALMONDS, CASHEWS, OR WALNUTS

¼ CUP (30 G) CACAO NIBS

3 TABLESPOONS POPPY SEEDS

A PINCH OF PINK HIMALAYAN SALT

⅓ CUP (½ STICK + 1½ TABLESPOONS; 75 G) UNSALTED BUTTER

½ CUP (170 G) HONEY

1 TABLESPOON ROSEWATER

¾ CUP (100 G) COARSELY CHOPPED DRIED SOUR CHERRIES, CURRANTS, CRANBERRIES, OR RASPBERRIES

A HANDFUL OF DRIED ROSE PETALS

lavender scones

makes nine scones

I like my scones to stand out in their own right and be strong, but submissive enough to be slathered. These are it. They're tender, light, and not too sweet, fragranced with just the right amount of lavender, which can often overpower or get buried. Serve warm, with jam and cream, or even dreamy lemon curd (page 227), for them at their finest.

Preheat the oven to 400°F (200°C). Line a large baking sheet with parchment paper.

Put the lavender and sugar into a small processor or grinder. Process until even and fragrant, a few seconds. Tip into a large bowl, along with the flour, baking powder, baking soda, and salt. Toss in the butter and use your fingers to rub it in until sandy. Form a well in the middle, then pour in the buttermilk, stirring with a wooden spoon, until just combined.

Tip the dough onto a floured work surface. Gather it up, giving it a few folds, and bring it together to form a 1-inch- (2.5-cm) thick mound. It'll be soft, so treat it gently and flour as needed to prevent it from sticking. Use a 2.5-inch (6-cm) round cutter to stamp out as many scones from the dough as possible, then place them onto the prepared sheet in rows of three, letting them almost touch. Reroll the scraps and repeat.

Bake for 18 to 20 minutes, until light golden brown. Let stand on the sheet for a few minutes before transferring to a wire rack to cool further, before serving.

½ TABLESPOON DRIED LAVENDER

½ CUP (100 G) GRANULATED SUGAR

3 CUPS (375 G) ALL-PURPOSE FLOUR, *PLUS EXTRA FOR DUSTING*

1 TABLESPOON BAKING POWDER

¾ TEASPOON BAKING SODA

½ TEASPOON SALT

½ CUP (1 STICK; 115 G) UNSALTED BUTTER, *COLD AND CUT INTO ½-INCH (12-MM) CUBES*

1 CUP + 2 TABLESPOONS (270 ML) BUTTERMILK

triple bean vanilla ice cream

serves four to six

This is nothing but pure, unadulterated vanilla ice cream. The flavor is
infused three pods deep and not faint at all; rich, with floral nuances. I think
we forget that vanilla is a flower, or part of it is at least—coming from the
ovaries of an orchid. Let it stand for a few minutes before you eat it, for the
creamiest, soft-serve–like texture.

Pour the cream and milk into a deep saucepan. Use a sharp knife to split
open the pods, then scrape out the seeds, adding them into the pan along
with the pods. Bring to a simmer over medium-low heat. Meanwhile, whisk
the yolks and sugar in a mixing bowl until pale and fluffy.

Slip a little stream of the hot cream into the yolks, whisking well to
acclimatize them to the heat, then pour it all into the saucepan set on the
stove. Continue to cook, stirring constantly, until it is thick enough to coat
the back of a spoon. It shouldn't take more than a few minutes. Remove
and stir in the salt. Pour into a large bowl, scraping out any seeds that
have stuck themselves to the bottom of the pan, then cover the surface
with plastic wrap to prevent a skin from forming. Chill until cold, at least
8 hours, but preferably overnight.

The next morning, fish out the pods and discard them. Churn in an
ice cream machine according to the manufacturer's instructions. It'll be
doubled, thick, and very creamy when it's done. Transfer into a container,
cover, and freeze until just firm before serving.

2 CUPS (480 ML) HEAVY CREAM

1¼ CUPS (300 ML) WHOLE MILK

3 VANILLA BEAN PODS

5 LARGE EGG YOLKS

¾ CUP (150 G) GRANULATED
SUGAR

A PINCH OF SALT

elderflower sabayon

serves six to eight

Sabayon is a sort of mousse-like custard, made with eggs, sugar, and alcohol, often wine. I use elderflower liqueur for it instead, which has a sweet floral headiness. It's not hard to find and I recommend sourcing it, if you can. There's a good amount in this recipe and you'll use it more than you'd think. It is strong, though, so keep that in mind if you go to lick the bowl. I don't want you swooning—at least not yet.

Put the egg yolks, sugar, liqueur, and lemon juice in a medium-size heatproof bowl. Give it a good stir to combine, then set the bowl over a saucepan filled with a few inches of barely simmering water. Do not allow the base of the bowl to touch the water below. Heat over medium-low heat, whisking constantly until it has thickened up enough to hold a trail if you run your finger through it, kind of like lemon curd, 8 to 10 minutes. Transfer to a bowl, covering the surface with plastic wrap to prevent a skin from forming, then chill until cold, at least 6 hours.

Just before you're ready to serve, whip the cream to soft peaks. Give the sabayon a stir to loosen it, then fold in the cream, gently. Serve soon after, keeping any leftovers cold.

6 LARGE EGG YOLKS

½ CUP + 2 TABLESPOONS (125 G) GRANULATED SUGAR

½ CUP (120 ML) ELDERFLOWER LIQUEUR

JUICE OF A SMALL LEMON

1¼ CUPS (300 ML) HEAVY CREAM

rhubarb and pink peppercorn tart

makes a 9-inch (23-cm) cake, which serves eight to twelve

I wouldn't call this a tart, but it's not a cake either; rather, it falls somewhere between the two. The bones of it come from a Nigel Slater recipe, which I've made a lot over the years, using all kinds of fruits and florals. It's made with polenta too, so it's a bit brash and dense, but delicate when handled.

Preheat the oven to 350°F (180°C). Set a 14 x 5-inch (35 x 13-cm) rectangular tart pan with a removable base onto a baking sheet.

To make the rhubarb, put the rhubarb, sugar, water, lemon juice, and rosewater in a nonstick skillet set over medium-low heat. Cook, turning the rhubarb over often in the juices, until tender. Set aside to cool.

Next, make the cake. Put the flour, polenta, baking powder, pink peppercorns, lemon zest, salt, and granulated sugar in a food processor. Pulse to distribute, then toss in the butter. Again, pulse until a coarse breadcrumb-like texture has formed. Tip into a large bowl.

In a measuring cup, whisk together the egg and buttermilk, then pour into the bowl with the dry ingredients. Using a wooden spoon, begin to blend it in until a soft and crumbly dough has formed, being careful not to overmix. You want it to just clump together.

Tip two-thirds of the dough into the base of the prepared pan, spreading it into an even layer. Spoon the rhubarb over the dough, straining as much of it from the juices as possible. Crumble the remaining dough over the rhubarb. It's fine if the fruit isn't all covered—better, in fact, as it looks wonderful peeking through.

Bake for 20 to 25 minutes, until golden brown. Let cool in the pan before unmolding. It has a very tender crumb, so handle it with care. Flourish with confectioners' sugar and rose petals, if using, before serving.

FOR THE RHUBARB

2 CUPS (200 G) RHUBARB CHUNKS (¼ INCH/6 MM)

⅓ CUP (70 G) GRANULATED SUGAR

¼ CUP (60 ML) WATER

JUICE OF A LEMON

1 TABLESPOON ROSEWATER

FOR THE CAKE

2 CUPS (250 G) ALL-PURPOSE FLOUR

1 CUP (150 G) POLENTA

2 TEASPOONS BAKING POWDER

1 TEASPOON PINK PEPPERCORNS

ZEST OF A LEMON

¼ TEASPOON SALT

1 CUP (200 G) GRANULATED SUGAR

¾ CUP + 2 TABLESPOONS (1½ STICKS + 2 TABLESPOONS; 200 G) UNSALTED BUTTER, *COLD AND CUT INTO ½-INCH (12-MM) CUBES*

1 LARGE EGG

⅓ CUP (80 ML) BUTTERMILK

CONFECTIONERS' SUGAR, *FOR FINISHING*

ROSE PETALS, *OPTIONAL*

violet mousse

serves four to six

Violets are soft, but strong if you let them. They long for something with backbone, like chocolate, which is sweet but at the same time bitter and dark. The amount of violet oil called for is left to your discretion, as its strength will vary according to brand. A few drops should be more than enough.

Put the chocolate in a medium-size heatproof bowl set over a saucepan filled with a few inches of barely simmering water. Do not allow the base of the bowl to touch the water below. Heat, stirring often, until melted. Remove and set aside to cool.

In the bowl of a stand mixer fitted with the whisk attachment, whisk the cream and violet oil until soft peaks have formed. Transfer to the refrigerator to chill until needed.

Next, bring the sugar and water to a boil over medium heat. While it's coming to temperature, start whisking the yolks in the bowl of a stand mixer that's set on medium speed. As soon as the sugar water comes to a boil, remove from the heat and slowly stream the syrup down the sides of the bowl and into the yolks, whisking until incorporated. Turn the speed to high and continue to whisk until pale, thick, and doubled in volume, about 4 more minutes. The bowl should no longer be hot to the touch.

With a rubber spatula, fold a third of the cream into the chocolate to loosen it. Fold in another third, followed by the last third, until almost incorporated. It should be a bit streaky. Fold in the yolk mixture, a little at a time, being careful not to deflate it too much, as you want the mousse to be as aerated as possible. Spoon into a large bowl, then chill for a few hours until set before spooning out and serving.

1½ CUPS (255 G) FINELY CHOPPED DARK CHOCOLATE

1½ CUPS (360 ML) HEAVY CREAM

A FEW DROPS VIOLET OIL

⅓ CUP (70 G) GRANULATED SUGAR

¼ CUP (60 ML) WATER

4 LARGE EGG YOLKS

sea salt violet cupcakes

makes twelve cupcakes

I don't make cupcakes often, but when I do, it's for celebration. They're a true party thing, a heft of frosting over dense chocolate cake. I like to use Swiss or Italian buttercream, as it's silkier, richer, and, I think, more refined, but there's something about the grit of American that's important for cake like this. I've enhanced it, though, using chocolate and salt, as well as violet oil, with the amount used left up to your discretion, as it can be quite strong.

Preheat the oven to 350°F (180°C). Line a twelve-cup cupcake pan with paper liners.

For the cupcakes, put the chocolate into a medium-size bowl, then pour the hot water over it. Let the mixture sit for a minute to acclimatize, then stir until melted. Set aside to cool.

Next, whisk together the flour, cocoa, baking soda, baking powder, and salt in a large mixing bowl. Stir in the sugar. In a large measuring cup, combine the egg, vanilla, buttermilk, and oil. Make a well in the center of the dry ingredients and stream in the liquids, whisking, until smooth. Pour in a bit of the melted chocolate mixture, whisking it in to loosen, then whisk in the rest until a thin batter has formed. Use a small measuring cup to scoop it out and into the cups, filling them about halfway.

Bake for 15 to 20 minutes, until just firm to the touch. A skewer inserted into the middle should come out clean. Let the cupcakes cool for 15 minutes before removing them from the pan and setting onto a wire rack to cool completely before frosting.

To make the buttercream, put the chocolate in a small heatproof bowl set over a saucepan filled with a few inches of barely simmering water. Do not allow the base of the bowl to touch the water below. Heat, stirring often, until melted. Remove and set aside to cool.

Meanwhile, in the bowl of a stand mixer fitted with the paddle attachment, beat the butter on medium speed until malleable, about a minute. Pause mixing to scrape down the bottom and side of the bowl. Beat in the confectioners' sugar until creamy, 3 to 5 minutes. Beat in the chocolate, followed by the violet oil, cream, and plain salt until velvety.

Spread a generous amount of the buttercream on top of each cupcake, using an offset palette knife to swirl it out. Sprinkle with a pinch of the vanilla bean gray salt. Serve soon after.

FOR THE CUPCAKES

⅓ CUP + 1 TEASPOON (60 G) FINELY CHOPPED DARK CHOCOLATE

½ CUP (120 ML) HOT WATER

½ CUP (65 G) ALL-PURPOSE FLOUR

¼ CUP + 1 TABLESPOON (30 G) DUTCH PROCESSED COCOA POWDER

¾ TEASPOON BAKING SODA

¼ TEASPOON BAKING POWDER

¼ TEASPOON SALT

¾ CUP + 2 TEASPOONS (160 G) GRANULATED SUGAR

1 LARGE EGG

1 TEASPOON VANILLA EXTRACT

⅓ CUP + 1½ TABLESPOONS (100 ML) BUTTERMILK

⅓ CUP + 1 TEASPOON (80 ML) VEGETABLE OIL

FOR THE BUTTERCREAM

¾ CUP (130 G) FINELY CHOPPED DARK CHOCOLATE

¾ CUP (1½ STICKS; 170 G) UNSALTED BUTTER, *SOFTENED AT ROOM TEMPERATURE*

1 CUP (120 G) CONFECTIONERS' SUGAR

A FEW DROPS VIOLET OIL

3 TABLESPOONS HEAVY CREAM

A PINCH OF SALT

VANILLA BEAN GRAY SALT (*SEE PAGE 229*), *FOR FINISHING*

mendiants

makes about eighty pieces

There's not much to a mendiant, other than melting chocolate and decorating with whatever you desire, but that's what makes them wonderful. You can be as creative as you'd like, using all kinds of things like flowers, fruits, nuts, salts, or sometimes gold leaf. It's hard to do them wrong, so adorn them as you please.

Put the chocolate into a large heatproof bowl set over a saucepan of barely simmering water. Do not allow the base of the bowl to touch the water below. Heat, stirring often, until melted. Remove and set aside to cool for about 5 minutes, to thicken up a little. Meanwhile, line a baking sheet with parchment paper.

Transfer the chocolate to a pastry bag and snip off the tip, then pipe out small, even-sized discs that are about 1½ inches (4 cm) in diameter on the sheet, forming a few at a time and adorning as you go. Alternatively, you could use a teaspoon to form them.

Chill until set, about 15 minutes, before serving. Pack leftovers in an airtight container with wax paper between the layers, and store at room temperature, or if it's too humid, in the refrigerator. They'll last for a week.

1½ CUPS (255 G) FINELY
CHOPPED DARK CHOCOLATE

CRYSTALLIZED OR DRIED
FLOWERS, NUTS, SEEDS,
DRIED FRUIT, CACAO NIBS,
FLEUR DE SEL, *FOR FINISHING*

frosted chamomile tea cake

makes an 8 x 4-inch (21 x 11-cm) loaf, which serves eight to ten

This is an afternoon cake, a rustic one, flavored softly with orange, honey, and chamomile. Though ideal for spring, it's the kind of cake that translates well across all seasons. You'll want to eat it all the time—in winter, alongside strong, milky tea, or as a picnic cake in summer.

Preheat the oven to 350°F (180°C). Grease and line an 8 x 4 x 3-inch (21 x 11 x 7-cm) loaf pan with parchment paper, leaving a slight overhang on both sides.

To make the cake, whisk together the flour, baking soda, salt, and chamomile tea leaves.

In the bowl of a stand mixer fitted with the paddle attachment, beat the butter and granulated sugar on medium speed until light and fluffy, 3 to 5 minutes. Pause to scrape down the bottom and side of the bowl. Add the eggs, one at a time, beating well to incorporate each addition, then beat in the vanilla and orange zest. Set the speed to low. Beat in half the dry ingredients, followed by all the sour cream, then beat in the remaining dry ingredients until aerated. Scrape the batter into the prepared pan.

Bake for 45 to 55 minutes, until golden brown. A skewer inserted into the middle should come out clean. Let cool in the pan for 15 minutes before lifting it out and onto a wire rack to cool completely before frosting.

To make the frosting, put the butter, confectioners' sugar, honey, vanilla, and salt in the bowl of a stand mixer fitted with the paddle attachment. Beat on medium speed until creamy, then add the mascarpone and beat until fluffy. Slather the frosting over the cake then serve soon after.

FOR THE CAKE

½ CUP + 1 TABLESPOON (1 STICK + 1 TABLESPOON; 130 G) UNSALTED BUTTER, *SOFTENED AT ROOM TEMPERATURE, PLUS EXTRA FOR GREASING THE PAN*

1½ CUPS (190 G) ALL-PURPOSE FLOUR

1 TEASPOON BAKING SODA

½ TEASPOON SALT

2 TEASPOONS CHAMOMILE TEA LEAVES

¾ CUP + 1 TABLESPOON (165 G) GRANULATED SUGAR

2 LARGE EGGS

1 TEASPOON VANILLA EXTRACT

ZEST OF AN ORANGE

½ CUP + 1 TABLESPOON (135 G) SOUR CREAM

FOR THE FROSTING

½ CUP (1 STICK; 115 G) UNSALTED BUTTER, *SOFTENED AT ROOM TEMPERATURE*

1 CUP (120 G) CONFECTIONERS' SUGAR

3 TABLESPOONS HONEY

½ TEASPOON VANILLA EXTRACT

A PINCH OF SALT

⅓ CUP (75 G) MASCARPONE, *AT ROOM TEMPERATURE*

white rose cake

makes an 8-inch (20-cm) cake, which serves eight to twelve

There's nothing more wonderful than a white rose. Ethereal, pure, and delicate, they're a pleasure. The same is true for this cake. The rose is present, but subtle, residing in the background, sighing, as it should. It's an innocent thing, and I think it's best to let it be just that.

Preheat the oven to 350°F (180°C). Grease and line three 8-inch (20-cm) round cake pans with parchment paper.

For the cake, combine the flour, baking powder, salt, and sugar in the bowl of a stand mixer fitted with the paddle attachment. Beat in the butter, a tablespoon at a time, until a sandy, meal-like texture has formed, about 3 minutes. Meanwhile, stir together the egg whites, milk, vanilla, and zest in a large measuring cup. In a slow stream, add half of the liquids to the beating mixture until just combined, then add in the rest. Turn the speed to high. Continue to beat until light and aerated. Divide among the prepared pans.

Bake for 25 to 30 minutes, rotating the pans halfway through, until golden brown. A skewer inserted into the middle should come out clean. Let the cakes cool in the pans for 15 minutes, before turning them out onto a wire rack to cool completely. Use a sharp serrated knife to level off any domed tops, if needed.

To make the syrup, put the sugar and water in a small saucepan. Heat, stirring often, until the sugar has dissolved. Brush it over the cakes to moisten.

For the buttercream, set the chocolate in a medium-size heatproof bowl set over a saucepan of barely simmering water. Do not let the base of the bowl touch the water below. Heat, stirring often, until melted. Remove and set aside to cool.

Next, put the egg whites and sugar into the bowl of a stand mixer. Set it over a saucepan filled with a few inches of barely simmering water.

FOR THE CAKE

2½ CUPS (315 G) CAKE FLOUR

1 TABLESPOON BAKING POWDER

½ TEASPOON SALT

1½ CUPS (300 G) GRANULATED SUGAR

¾ CUP + 1 TABLESPOON (1½ STICKS + 1 TABLESPOON; 185 G) UNSALTED BUTTER, *SOFTENED AT ROOM TEMPERATURE, PLUS EXTRA FOR GREASING THE PANS*

5 LARGE EGG WHITES

1 CUP + 2 TABLESPOONS (270 ML) WHOLE MILK

1 TABLESPOON VANILLA EXTRACT

ZEST OF A LEMON

FOR THE SYRUP

¼ CUP (50 G) GRANULATED SUGAR

3 TABLESPOONS WATER

FOR THE BUTTERCREAM

¾ CUP (130 G) FINELY CHOPPED WHITE CHOCOLATE

5 EGG WHITES

1 CUP + 2 TEASPOONS (210 G) GRANULATED SUGAR

1½ CUPS + 1 TEASPOON (3 STICKS + 1 TEASPOON; 350 G) UNSALTED BUTTER, *SOFTENED AT ROOM TEMPERATURE*

¼ CUP (60 G) CRÈME FRAÎCHE (*SEE PAGE 225*)

1 TABLESPOON ROSEWATER

Do not let the base of the bowl touch the water below. Heat, whisking often, until it reaches 160°F (71°C) on a candy thermometer. The sugar should be dissolved and the mixture hot to the touch. Set the bowl onto the stand mixer fitted with the whisk attachment and whisk on high speed until thick and glossy, about 5 to 7 minutes. Switch out the whisk for the paddle attachment. Beat in the butter, a tablespoon at a time, until it is all used up, then slowly stream in the chocolate, followed by the crème fraiche, and rosewater. Continue to beat until a silky-smooth buttercream has formed.

When you're ready to assemble, put the first cake layer, top facing up, onto a plate. Spread a few generous tablespoons of the buttercream almost to the edges with an offset palette knife. Add the next cake layer, frosting in the same manner, followed by the final cake layer. Cover the top and sides with buttercream then chill until set, at least 20 minutes. It's best eaten on the day of making but can be kept covered in the refrigerator for up to 3 days.

rose walnut
chocolate chip cookies

makes sixteen to twenty cookies

I've always thought that adding anything but chocolate to cookies was sacrilegious, but then I made these and that changed. They're seductive and musky—perfumed, but not overly so. If you aren't a fan of rose, it can hit you on the nose a bit, so I would recommend using half the amount and going from there. They're amorous.

Whisk together the flour, baking powder, baking soda, and salt.

Put the butter into a medium-size saucepan set over medium-low heat. Heat, stirring often, until melted. Pour into a large bowl then add in the sugars and whisk until combined. Whisk in the egg, followed by the rosewater and vanilla. Tip in the dry ingredients. Beat with a wooden spoon until a soft dough has just begun to form, then mix in the chocolate and walnuts. Cover and chill until firm, 30 minutes.

Meanwhile, set racks in the lower and upper thirds of an oven. Preheat to 350°F (180°C). Line two baking sheets with parchment paper.

Using a scoop or tablespoon as a measure, portion out evenly sized amounts of the dough. If you're using a spoon, use your hands to roll them into balls. Divide between the prepared sheets, placing them a few inches apart for spreading. You should be able to fit 8 to 10 per sheet. Sprinkle with a little fleur de sel. You can set leftover dough balls aside to be baked off later, or, store in an airtight container and freeze for up to 2 months. Allow to stand at room temperature for about 15 minutes before baking from frozen.

Bake for 10 to 12 minutes, rotating the sheets between the upper and lower thirds of the oven halfway through, until golden, the edges crisp, but the centers still soft. Let the cookies stand on the sheets for a few minutes, before transferring them onto a wire rack to cool further, before serving.

2¼ CUPS (280 G) ALL-PURPOSE FLOUR

1 TEASPOON BAKING POWDER

½ TEASPOON BAKING SODA

½ TEASPOON SALT

⅔ CUP (1¼ STICKS + 1 TEASPOON; 150 G) UNSALTED BUTTER

¾ CUP + 1 TEASPOON (170 G) LIGHT BROWN SUGAR

½ CUP (100 G) GRANULATED SUGAR

1 LARGE EGG

1 TABLESPOON ROSEWATER

2 TEASPOONS VANILLA EXTRACT

1 CUP (170 G) COARSELY CHOPPED DARK CHOCOLATE

½ CUP (70 G) CHOPPED WALNUTS

FLEUR DE SEL, *FOR FINISHING*

ROSE PETALS, *OPTIONAL*

orange blossom crème caramel

serves eight to twelve

If I were to go out, brilliantly, it would be with crème caramel. I only ever make it on special occasions, and this recipe is one that has long served me best. It's an end-all—rich, creamy, and dulcet, and if you catch it at the right moment, vulnerable. You'll want to start it early, at least half a day in advance, as it needs time to settle. The longer it sits, the better.

Preheat the oven to 300°F (150°C). Set a mold that holds about 5 cups (1.2 L) in a roasting pan. Bring a large kettle of water to a boil.

First, make the caramel. Put 1 cup (200 g) of the sugar in a deep saucepan set over medium heat. Cook, swirling often but not stirring, until it has turned into an amber-hued liquid. Be sure to watch it carefully, as it can go from fine to black in an instant. Immediately pour into the mold and set aside to harden.

Next, make the custard. In a large bowl, combine the milk and cream. In a measuring cup, whisk together the eggs, orange blossom water, vanilla seeds, and remaining ⅓ cup (70 g) of sugar. Stream the egg mixture into the bowl with the milk, whisking slowly, until combined. Strain through a fine-mesh sieve and into the mold (still in the roasting pan), skimming off any froth that has formed on the top. Tent with aluminum foil then pour enough of the boiling-hot water into the pan until it reaches halfway up the sides of the mold.

Bake for about an hour, until just set but with a wobble to it in the center. Remove the mold from the water and cool to room temperature. Chill for at least 6 hours, but preferably overnight.

When you're ready to serve, set the mold into a few inches of hot water to melt the top, then run a warm knife around the edges to loosen it. Invert onto a rimmed plate, letting it sit upside down for a minute to release itself, then remove the mold. Serve soon after, coated in spoonfuls of caramel.

1 ⅓ CUPS (270 G) GRANULATED SUGAR

1 ½ CUPS (360 ML) WHOLE MILK

1 ½ CUPS (360 ML) HEAVY CREAM

6 LARGE EGGS

2 TEASPOONS ORANGE BLOSSOM WATER

SEEDS OF A VANILLA POD

chamomile shortbread

makes ten pieces

The flavor of chamomile is like a long, slow whisper. It's one of the less heady florals, soft, soothing, and mellow, never a scream. You can't force it; it has to come to you, and it will, in its own time. If you don't have dried flowers, tea leaves can be used instead.

Preheat the oven to 325°F (160°C). Grease and line an 8-inch (20 cm) square baking pan with parchment paper, leaving a slight overhang on the sides.

Sift together the flour, rice flour, and salt, then stir in the chamomile.

In the bowl of a stand mixer fitted with the paddle attachment, cream the butter on medium speed until smooth, about a minute. Add the sugar and beat until pale and creamy, then beat in the vanilla and zest. Lower the mixer speed and tip in the dry ingredients. Beat until a soft dough has just begun to form—there should still be some unworked pockets of flour throughout—then mix in the chocolate. Tip into the prepared pan, using the back of a spoon to press it into an even layer. Sprinkle the top with a little extra sugar.

Bake for 30 to 35 minutes, until light golden brown. Remove and immediately use a sharp knife to score it into ten rectangular fingers. Let cool before lifting out and serving.

1 CUP (2 STICKS; 230 G) UNSALTED BUTTER, *SOFTENED AT ROOM TEMPERATURE, PLUS EXTRA FOR GREASING THE PAN*

1¾ CUPS + 1½ TABLESPOONS (230 G) ALL-PURPOSE FLOUR

⅓ CUP + 1½ TABLESPOONS (65 G) RICE FLOUR

½ TEASPOON SALT

1 TABLESPOON DRIED CHAMOMILE FLOWERS

½ CUP (100 G) GRANULATED SUGAR, *PLUS MORE FOR THE TOP*

1 TEASPOON VANILLA EXTRACT

ZEST OF A LEMON

½ CUP (85 G) COARSELY CHOPPED WHITE CHOCOLATE

rose macaroon cake

makes a 9-inch (23-cm) cake, which serves eight to twelve

This is one of the more unusual recipes in this book, because of the cake's crisp and fractured top. It is delicate, though, and as such should be treated with care. Because of the meringue, it'll be hard to tell if the cake beneath is done, so allow your senses to guide you. It should be light fawn in color, split, and fragrant.

Preheat the oven to 350°F (180°C). Grease and line a 9-inch (23-cm) round cake pan with parchment paper.

To make the cake, sift together the flour, baking powder, and salt.

In the bowl of a stand mixer fitted with the paddle attachment, cream the butter and sugar on medium speed until pale and fluffy, 3 to 5 minutes. Pause mixing to scrape down the bottom and side of the bowl. Add the eggs, one at a time, beating well to incorporate each addition, then beat in the vanilla. Set the mixer speed to low. Beat in half of the dry ingredients, followed by all of the crème fraîche, then the remaining dry ingredients, until light and aerated. Fold in the coconut, then scrape into the prepared pan.

Next, make the meringue. Put the egg whites into a clean bowl of a stand mixer fitted with the whisk attachment. Whisk on medium speed until foamy, then add in the sugar, a tablespoon at a time, until it is all used up. Continue to whisk until thick and glossy, then whisk in the rosewater. Spoon then swirl the meringue on top of the batter.

Bake for 45 to 50 minutes, until the top is crackled and the color of light fawn. Let the cake cool for about 15 minutes, before transferring it out and onto a wire rack to cool completely. Finish with a dusting of confectioners' sugar and rose petals, if using.

FOR THE CAKE

⅔ CUP (1¼ STICKS + 1 TEASPOON; 150 G) UNSALTED BUTTER, *SOFTENED AT ROOM TEMPERATURE, PLUS EXTRA FOR GREASING THE PAN*

1½ CUPS + 1½ TABLESPOONS (200 G) ALL-PURPOSE FLOUR

1 TEASPOON BAKING POWDER

½ TEASPOON SALT

1 CUP + 2 TABLESPOONS (225 G) GRANULATED SUGAR

3 LARGE EGGS

1 TEASPOON VANILLA EXTRACT

½ CUP (120 G) CRÈME FRAÎCHE *(SEE PAGE 225)*

½ CUP + 1½ TABLESPOONS (50 G) UNSWEETENED SHREDDED COCONUT

FOR THE MERINGUE

2 LARGE EGG WHITES

1 CUP (200 G) GRANULATED SUGAR

1 TABLESPOON ROSEWATER

CONFECTIONERS' SUGAR, *FOR FINISHING*

ROSE PETALS, *OPTIONAL*

BRAMBLE

"Please, devour me."

—MARGUERITE DURAS, *Hiroshima Mon Amour*

SOME THINK THAT WINTER is for hibernation, but for me, it's the summer. It's meant for our fever. One long delirium is how I remember it best. Of being devoured, how night felt, how it might as well have been day, the fireflies, all the things I should know, and all the things I shouldn't, how it hurt, but how the hurt felt wonderful, summer.

I will never love it as much as I do the cold, the dark. But I am learning, slowly, like how the season goes. For the summers aren't short. They're long and pervasive, ruthless. The heat stifles and often I feel as if I can't breathe. But that too can be wonderful. Anything to make the body sing.

There's a certain kind of pleasure that comes with eating in the summer. It's less fussed, with a greater focus on produce, time, and flavor. When I bake, it's in the early hours. The oven gets turned on, thought off. Windows open, to let the outside in. It starts to feel like a race against the inevitable, for in a few hours, the sun will be up, and it'll be over.

The flavors of summer aren't a linger or laze, but a slap, so palpable, bodied, and full of burst, that it's a shock. It's berries that mark the season. Sticky, sweet, and stained, to taste them seems a sin. But like the brambles that surround them, their sweetness comes with a sting.

I like the tart ones best. The kind that pucker and are yet to peak, that need a bit of warmth to bring them out. I don't like to treat them too much, rather, allowing their nature to shine, like they once did, under the sun.

There's a particular tart that I make when the weather warms. It's filled with berries, in shades of pink, purple, black, and red. It never ends up the same. Sometimes, the fruit isn't sweet, so there's a heavier dust of sugar at the end, or at others, it's too sweet, then there's a need for crème fraîche, to cut through.

And that's how it should be. The summer, never faithful.

ganache thumbprints

makes twenty-eight cookies

It may not seem like a lot, but something as small as a tablespoon holds power. At least that's how I feel about these. Their flavor reminds me of those little bottle-shaped liqueur chocolates that somehow we all grew up with—robust, boozy, and rich, with a body that does nothing but disintegrate. The liqueur comes last. It's not strong, but it'll seep into you, slowly, especially if you have more than one. There's a good chance of that.

Set oven racks in the lower and upper thirds of the oven. Preheat to 350°F (180°C). Line two large baking sheets with parchment paper.

For the dough, whisk together the flour, cocoa, and salt.

In the bowl of a stand mixer fitted with the paddle attachment, beat the butter and sugar on medium speed until creamy, 3 minutes. Pause mixing to scrape down the bottom and side of the bowl. Add in the egg yolks, one at a time, beating well to incorporate each addition, then mix in the vanilla. Lower the speed and tip in the dry ingredients. Beat until a soft dough has just begun to form, no more than 30 seconds.

Tip the sanding sugar into a shallow bowl. Using a tablespoon as a measure, scoop the dough out and into even-size portions, rolling them into smooth balls. If you have a scale, they should each weigh about 25 g. Roll in the sugar, then divide between the prepared sheets, placing them a few inches apart for spreading. With your thumb, make a small well-like indent in the middle of each, not pushing so far down that you touch the bottom.

Bake for 10 to 12 minutes, rotating the pans top to bottom and bottom to top halfway through, until crackled. The indents will have puffed up a bit, so as soon as you remove the trays, push them down again, lightly. I do it with my finger, but you can also use the end of a wooden spoon if the cookies are too hot. Transfer off the sheet and onto a wire rack to cool completely.

Meanwhile, make the ganache. Put the chocolate into a medium-size heatproof bowl. Pour the cream into a small saucepan and bring to a simmer over medium heat. Stream it over the chocolate. Stir slowly, until smooth, then stir in the crème de cassis. Leave to stand for a few minutes to thicken up slightly, then spoon into the thumbprints. Serve once the ganache has set. They're best eaten on the day of making but can be stored in an airtight container at room temperature for up to 3 days.

FOR THE DOUGH

2 CUPS (250 G) ALL-PURPOSE FLOUR

¾ CUP (75 G) DUTCH PROCESSED COCOA POWDER

½ TEASPOON SALT

1 CUP (2 STICKS; 230 G) UNSALTED BUTTER, *SOFTENED AT ROOM TEMPERATURE*

1 CUP (200 G) GRANULATED SUGAR

2 LARGE EGG YOLKS

1 TEASPOON VANILLA EXTRACT

¼ CUP (50 G) GRANULATED SUGAR, *FOR SANDING*

FOR THE GANACHE

1 CUP + 1 TABLESPOON (180 G) FINELY CHOPPED DARK CHOCOLATE

½ CUP (120 ML) HEAVY CREAM

1 TABLESPOON CRÈME DE CASSIS

blackcurrant opera cake

makes an 8-inch (20-cm) cake, which serves eight to twelve

I don't like to bake cakes in the heat, but this one I do. The layers take barely any time and are so light that you could hardly call it cake, forgetting all the buttercream and ganache, of course. It's intriguing too, using sweet and sticky crème de cassis, a blackcurrant-flavored liqueur that, oddly, pairs well with coffee. Add chocolate and it gets even better. You'll notice it.

Preheat the oven to 350°F (180°C). Line three 8-inch (20-cm) round cake pans with parchment paper.

First, make the cake. In the bowl of a stand mixer fitted with the whisk attachment, whisk the eggs and confectioners' sugar on medium speed until pale, thick, and almost doubled in volume, 3 minutes. It should be able to hold a trail when the whisk is raised, before flowing softly back onto itself. Sift the flour over the mixture, then add the hazelnuts and fold until almost combined (it should still be a bit streaky), then fold in the butter.

In a separate bowl, whisk the whites on medium speed until foamy. Add in the granulated sugar, a bit at a time, until it is all used up. Raise the speed and continue to whisk until a stiff and glossy meringue has formed. Using large, guiding strokes, fold a third of it into the hazelnut mixture to loosen it, then fold in another third, followed by the last, until just combined. Divide among the prepared pans, smoothing it out with an offset palette knife.

Bake for 8 to 10 minutes, until the cakes spring back when pressed. Remove and let cool for about 15 minutes, before turning out and onto a wire rack to cool completely. Use a sharp serrated knife to slice them in half horizontally so that you have six even layers.

To make the syrup, put the water, granulated sugar, and espresso powder in a small saucepan. Bring to a boil, stirring often, until dissolved. Drench the cakes with the syrup.

FOR THE CAKE

3 LARGE EGGS

1 CUP (120 G) CONFECTIONERS' SUGAR

¼ CUP (30 G) ALL-PURPOSE FLOUR

1¼ CUPS (120 G) GROUND HAZELNUTS

2 TABLESPOONS UNSALTED BUTTER, *MELTED*

3 LARGE EGG WHITES

¼ CUP (50 G) GRANULATED SUGAR

FOR THE SYRUP

¼ CUP (60 ML) WATER

¼ CUP (50 G) GRANULATED SUGAR

1 TEASPOON ESPRESSO POWDER

Next, make the ganache. Put the chocolate in a medium bowl. In a small saucepan, bring the cream to a boil, then remove and pour it all over the chocolate. Let the mixture sit for a minute to acclimatize, then stir until smooth. Stir in the crème de cassis and butter. Set aside until the ganache has thickened up enough to spread.

Last, make the buttercream. Put the granulated sugar and water in a medium-size saucepan and heat on high until it reaches 250°F (120°C) on a candy thermometer. It should be at a boil and the sugar dissolved. Meanwhile, put the yolks into the bowl of a stand mixer fitted with the whisk attachment. Start whisking them, on medium speed, until pale. Once the syrup has reached temperature, stream it slowly into the yolks. Increase the speed and whisk until thick and glossy, 3 to 5 minutes. The bowl should no longer be hot to the touch. Switch out the whisk for the paddle attachment, then beat in the butter, a tablespoon at a time, until it is all used up. Add in the coffee and salt. Continue to beat until a silky-smooth buttercream has formed, a few more minutes.

To assemble the cake, put the first layer onto a serving plate. Spread on a few tablespoons of buttercream, then top with another cake layer, pressing it down lightly. Spread on a few tablespoons of ganache, almost to the edges. Top again with another cake layer. Repeat this layering process until all the cake has been used up.

Chill until just set, 20 minutes, then cover the top of the cake with the remaining ganache. Again, chill to set, then use a sharp knife to trim off the edges to reveal the layers. The cake is best eaten on the day of making but can be kept for up to 3 days in the refrigerator.

FOR THE GANACHE

1 ¼ CUPS (215 G) FINELY CHOPPED DARK CHOCOLATE

½ CUP (120 ML) HEAVY CREAM

¼ CUP (60 ML) CRÈME DE CASSIS

1 TABLESPOON UNSALTED BUTTER

FOR THE BUTTERCREAM

⅓ CUP (70 G) GRANULATED SUGAR

2 TABLESPOONS WATER

3 LARGE EGG YOLKS

¾ CUP + 1 TEASPOON (1½ STICKS + 1 TEASPOON; 175 G) UNSALTED BUTTER, *SOFTENED AT ROOM TEMPERATURE*

1 TABLESPOON ESPRESSO POWDER MIXED WITH 1 TABLESPOON HOT WATER

A PINCH OF SALT

almond paste cakes

makes twelve cakes

These are like friends, but made with almond paste. They're nutty, moist, and damp, studded with blackberries too. You could use any other type of fruit, depending on what's in season, and I've even left fruit out altogether, and made them with nuts and spices, for a winter version.

Preheat the oven to 325°F (160°C). Grease a twelve-cup financier mold or muffin pan with the extra butter.

Whisk together the flour, baking powder, and salt.

Break up the almond paste, then add it into the bowl of a stand mixer fitted with the paddle attachment, along with the sugar. Beat, on medium speed, until clumpy, then add in the butter. Beat to form a fluffy paste, 3 minutes, then pause mixing to scrape down the bottom and side of the bowl. In a separate small bowl, whisk the egg whites together to loosen. Add them to the mixer bowl and beat until well combined, then beat in the almond extract. Add in the dry ingredients, turn the speed to medium-high, and continue to beat until aerated. Fold in the blackberries. Spoon into the molds, filling them no more than two-thirds full, then scatter the tops with almonds.

Bake for 20 to 25 minutes, until golden brown and springy to the touch. The time it takes will likely depend on the type of pan you're using, so keep a watchful eye on them as they near done. Let cool in the pan for 15 minutes, then run a blunt knife around their edges, easing the cakes out carefully and onto a wire rack. Dust with confectioners' sugar before serving.

½ CUP + 1 TABLESPOON (1 STICK + 1 TABLESPOON; 130 G) UNSALTED BUTTER, *SOFTENED AT ROOM TEMPERATURE, PLUS EXTRA FOR GREASING THE PAN*

¾ CUP (90 G) ALL-PURPOSE FLOUR

1 TEASPOON BAKING POWDER

¼ TEASPOON SALT

1 CUP (260 G) ALMOND PASTE (*SEE PAGE 223*)

¾ CUP + 2 TABLESPOONS (175 G) GRANULATED SUGAR

5 LARGE EGG WHITES

1 TEASPOON ALMOND EXTRACT

1 CUP (145 G) BLACKBERRIES

A HANDFUL OF SLICED ALMONDS, *FOR THE TOP*

CONFECTIONERS' SUGAR, *FOR FINISHING*

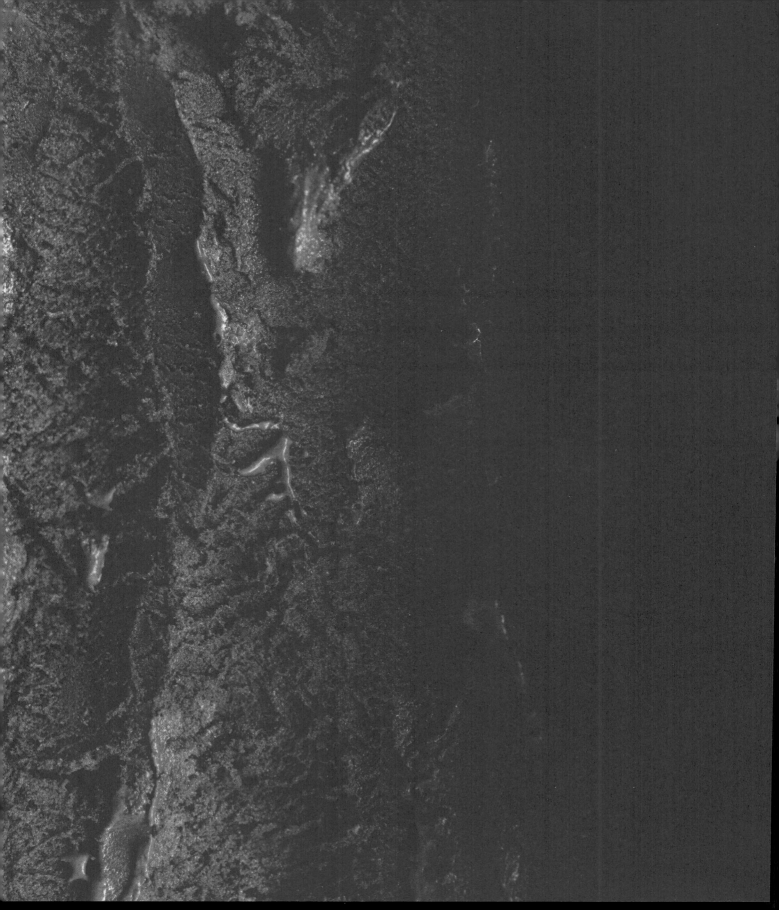

chocolate cassis ice cream

serves four to six

Crème de cassis is a sticky-sweet liqueur made from blackcurrants. It's syruplike, cloyingly so, with a taste of darkness. Because of how potent it is, it pairs well with other things of strength, like chocolate. There's a good amount of it in this ice cream, but I think that's fine, given how intense it's meant to be. Savor, don't savage it.

Put the chocolate into a large bowl, setting it aside but near to the space where you'll be working.

Pour the milk into a large saucepan. Heat, over medium-low, until it comes to a simmer. Meanwhile, whisk the egg yolks, sugar, and cocoa until thick in a medium-size heatproof bowl.

Slip a little stream of the hot milk into the yolks, whisking well to acclimatize them to the heat, then pour it all into the saucepan set on the stove. Continue to cook, stirring constantly, until it is thick enough to coat the back of a spoon. Do not allow it to come to a boil.

Remove from the heat and pour into the bowl with the chocolate, letting it sit for a minute to adjust, then stir until the chocolate is melted. Stir in the crème de cassis. Cover with plastic wrap, pressing it onto the surface to prevent a skin from forming. Chill until cold, at least 8 hours but preferably overnight.

When you're ready to churn, give the mixture a good stir to loosen, as it'll have thickened up overnight. Transfer to an ice cream machine and churn according to the manufacturer's instructions. It'll be thick, creamy, and near doubled in volume when it's done. Scrape into a container, cover, and freeze until just firm before serving.

1 CUP + 3 TABLESPOONS (200 G) FINELY CHOPPED DARK CHOCOLATE

3 CUPS (720 ML) WHOLE MILK

6 LARGE EGG YOLKS

¾ CUP (150 G) GRANULATED SUGAR

¼ CUP + 2½ TABLESPOONS (40 G) DUTCH PROCESSED COCOA POWDER

¼ CUP (60 ML) CRÈME DE CASSIS

blueberry almond scones

makes eight scones

I will never tire of making scones; their possibilities are endless. These are my ideal summer rendition. They're filled with blueberries and sweet pockets of white chocolate and are tender because of a base of almond and crème fraîche. Eat them while they're still warm and the chocolate melted.

Line two large baking sheets with parchment paper.

In a measuring cup, give the crème fraîche, cream, and vanilla a good stir together until smooth, then set it in the refrigerator to keep cold until needed.

Next, whisk the flour, ground almonds, baking powder, baking soda, salt, and sugar in a large mixing bowl. Add in the butter cubes and toss to coat. With a pastry blender or a metal spatula, cut in the butter until it is in mostly pea-size pieces. A few large stray chunks are fine to remain. Make a well in the center, then add the cream mixture, chocolate, and blueberries. With a wooden spoon, stir until a shaggy dough has begun to form. It shouldn't be well incorporated, but rough, with a few dry-floured pockets remaining throughout. Tip onto a lightly floured work surface.

Use your hands to bring the dough together, incorporating as much of the dry bits as possible. Pat into a rough mound that's about 1½ inches (4 cm) thick, then fold in half over itself, give it a quarter turn, and reshape. Repeat this process three more times until the dough has made a full rotation. It'll seem quite tender to handle at first, almost breakable, but it will come together as you continue to work it. Shape into a 1-inch- (2.5-cm) thick rectangle, then slice it into 8 evenly sized pieces. Place onto one of the baking sheets and freeze until firm, 20 minutes.

Meanwhile, set the oven racks in the lower and upper thirds of the oven. Preheat to 375°F (190°C).

When you're ready to bake, divide the scones between the sheets. Brush with the egg wash, then sprinkle with raw sugar.

Bake for 20 to 25 minutes, rotating halfway through, until golden brown. Let the scones stand on the sheet for a few minutes before transferring them off and onto a wire rack to cool further before serving.

⅔ CUP (160 G) CRÈME FRAÎCHE (*SEE PAGE 225*)

⅓ CUP (80 ML) HEAVY CREAM

1 TEASPOON VANILLA EXTRACT

2¼ CUPS + 1 TEASPOON (285 G) ALL-PURPOSE FLOUR, *PLUS EXTRA FOR THE WORK SURFACE*

1 CUP + 2 TEASPOONS (100 G) GROUND ALMONDS

2 TEASPOONS BAKING POWDER

½ TEASPOON BAKING SODA

½ TEASPOON SALT

⅓ CUP (70 G) GRANULATED SUGAR

¾ CUP + 1½ TABLESPOONS (1½ STICKS + 1½ TABLESPOONS; 190 G) UNSALTED BUTTER, *COLD AND CUT INTO ½-INCH (12-MM) CUBES*

⅔ CUP (115 G) COARSELY CHOPPED WHITE CHOCOLATE

2 CUPS (200 G) BLUEBERRIES

1 LARGE EGG, *LIGHTLY BEATEN FOR THE EGG WASH*

RAW SUGAR, *FOR FINISHING*

raspberry blondies

makes nine to twelve blondies

When you've got something as sweet as a blondie, balancing is needed. Raspberries are perfect, as they have a sharpness that's rather sedating, and contain rosy, citrusy, and green notes too, which add depth to something that's often one-dimensional. Use fresh, not frozen raspberries here—the latter have too much moisture.

Preheat the oven to 350°F (180°C). Grease and line an 8-inch (20-cm) square baking pan with parchment paper, allowing an overhang on the sides.

First, brown the butter. Put it into a deep saucepan set over medium heat, stirring often, until melted. Turn the heat to medium-high and continue to cook, swirling the pan often but not stirring, until a deep-amber-hued liquid has formed. It will foam, hiss, and crackle but should subside as it nears done. Pour into a large bowl, scraping in any burnt bits that have formed at the base of the pan, then whisk in the sugar. Add the egg, whisk until combined, then whisk in the vanilla until glossy.

Set a fine-mesh sieve over the bowl. Sift in the flour, baking powder, and salt, folding with a large rubber spatula until just combined. Fold in the raspberries, white chocolate, and almonds. Scrape it into the prepared pan, using an offset palette knife to smooth it into an even layer. Sprinkle with fleur de sel.

Bake for 22 to 25 minutes, until the top is golden, crackled, and shiny. The edges should be firm and the middle just set, but still slightly gooey. Let cool in the pan completely before lifting out and slicing into squares. The blondies will keep well, covered on the counter, for up to 3 days.

½ CUP + 1 TABLESPOON (1 STICK + 1 TABLESPOON; 130 G) UNSALTED BUTTER, *PLUS EXTRA FOR GREASING THE PAN*

1 CUP (220 G) LIGHT BROWN SUGAR

1 LARGE EGG

1 TABLESPOON VANILLA EXTRACT

1 CUP (125 G) ALL-PURPOSE FLOUR

1 TEASPOON BAKING POWDER

½ TEASPOON SALT

1 CUP (125 G) FRESH RASPBERRIES

⅔ CUP (115 G) COARSELY CHOPPED WHITE CHOCOLATE

½ CUP (60 G) COARSELY CHOPPED BLANCHED ALMONDS

FLEUR DE SEL, *FOR FINISHING*

boysenberry frozen yogurt

serves four

Forget the thought that this will be like ice cream, because it won't.
It's sharper, tangier, and icier, and all about the fruit too. I grew up with
boysenberries, and for me, they're one of the most potent and perfumed of
all fruit, coming second to blackcurrants. They're naturally very sweet, and
riper ones will make for an even sweeter yogurt, so keep that in mind before
you start. I sometimes add in a bit more zest, depending.

Put the boysenberries, sugar, and lemon juice into a medium-size saucepan
set over medium-low heat. Cook, stirring often, until the berries have slumped
and the liquid has transformed into a thick and sticky syrup, 5 to 7 minutes.
Set aside to cool.

Meanwhile, in the bowl of a stand mixer fitted with the whisk attachment,
whip the cream and vanilla to soft peaks, being cautious of taking it no
further. Transfer to the refrigerator to keep cold until needed.

Once the berries are cool, put them into a large bowl along with the
yogurt. Stir until combined, then fold in the cream. Churn in an ice cream
machine according to the manufacturer's instructions. It'll be thick and
creamy when it's done. Scrape into a container, then cover and freeze until
just set, before serving.

2¼ CUPS (300 G) BOYSENBERRIES

½ CUP (100 G) GRANULATED
SUGAR

JUICE OF A LEMON

¾ CUP (180 ML) HEAVY CREAM

1 TEASPOON VANILLA EXTRACT

1½ CUPS (360 G) NATURAL
YOGURT

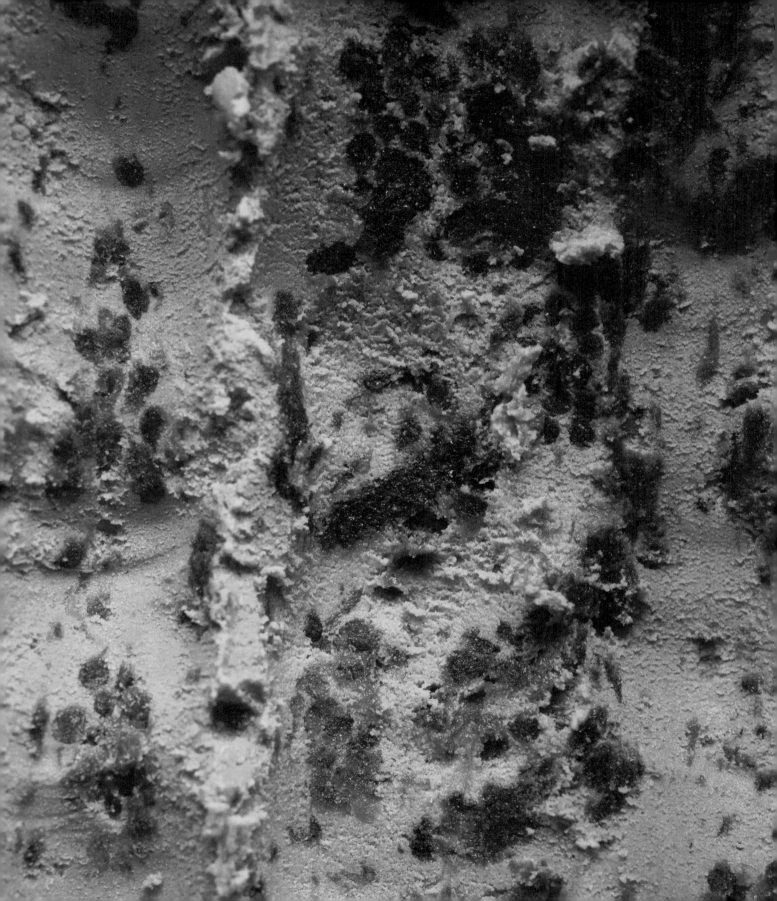

clafoutis

serves four

This isn't too fluffy, but dense, with a bodied pancake-like custard that suspends the fruit perfectly. You can have it cold, but I like it hot, as soon as it's out of the oven, still puffed. It will fall as soon as it's exposed to air, though, so if you want to keep it pious, serve it as soon as you can.

Preheat the oven to 400°F (200°C). Grease a large cast iron skillet with a little extra butter, then toss in some sugar, shaking, until well coated. Tap to remove the excess, then set aside.

First, make the clafoutis. Put the butter into a deep saucepan. Heat, stirring often, until golden and melted, then turn the heat to medium-high and continue to cook, swirling the pan often but not stirring, until an amber-hued liquid has formed. It will foam, hiss, and crackle at first, but subside as it nears done. Set aside to cool.

Put the eggs into a blender and blend on high speed until frothy, no more than 10 seconds. Any longer, and the custard runs the risk of ending up quite tough. Add in the flour, sugar, and milk, followed by the melted butter. Blend, again, until the batter is just combined, about 15 more seconds. Pour into the prepared skillet, then scatter in the currants.

Bake for 15 minutes. It'll have started to turn golden brown and the edges puffed up a bit too. Lower the oven temperature to 350°F (180°C). Continue to bake for another 15 to 20 minutes, until just set and puffed.

Meanwhile, make the syrup by bringing the sugar, lemon juice, and water to a boil over medium heat, stirring often to dissolve the sugar, until sticky and glossy. As soon as the clafoutis is done, drench it in the syrup and serve immediately.

FOR THE CLAFOUTIS

¼ CUP + 1 TABLESPOON (½ STICK + 1 TABLESPOON; 70 G) UNSALTED BUTTER, *PLUS EXTRA FOR GREASING THE DISH*

¼ CUP (50 G) GRANULATED SUGAR, *PLUS EXTRA FOR PREPARING THE DISH*

3 LARGE EGGS

⅓ CUP + 2 TABLESPOONS (60 G) ALL-PURPOSE FLOUR

⅔ CUP (160 ML) WHOLE MILK

1½ CUPS (150 G) BLACKCURRANTS

FOR THE SYRUP

⅓ CUP (70 G) GRANULATED SUGAR

JUICE OF A LEMON

2 TABLESPOONS WATER

currants and cream

serves four to six

There's not much else to this except sugar, cream, and fruit, enfolded—
similar to a fool in a way. Because of the white chocolate, it is a bit sweet, so
the tart, perfumed currants pair with it perfectly. It can be prepared ahead
of time and left to chill until you're ready to serve it; a lifesaver in the heat.

First, make the cream. Put the chocolate into a medium-size heatproof bowl.
In a medium-size saucepan, bring 1 cup (240 ml) of the cream to a boil, then
pour it over the chocolate. Let stand for a minute, then stir until smooth.
Cover with plastic wrap, pressing it onto the surface to prevent a skin from
forming. Transfer to the refrigerator and chill until cold, at least 6 hours.

Next, put the currants into a medium-size saucepan along with the sugar
and crème de cassis. Heat over medium-low heat until just slumped, being
careful not to let them lose their form completely. The juices should be thick
and syrup-like too. Like the cream, chill until cold.

When you're ready to serve, put the white chocolate cream into the bowl
of a stand mixer fitted with the whisk attachment, then add the remaining
cream. Whip to soft peaks. Fold in the currants softly, until streaked. The
less you fold, the more distinct the streak, so try to do it for as little as
possible—just enough to get them rippled through. Serve cold, soon after.

FOR THE CREAM

²/₃ CUP (115 G) FINELY CHOPPED
WHITE CHOCOLATE

1 ²/₃ CUPS (400 ML) HEAVY CREAM

FOR THE CURRANTS

1 ¼ CUPS (125 G)
BLACKCURRANTS

¼ CUP (50 G) GRANULATED
SUGAR

2 TABLESPOONS CRÈME DE
CASSIS

frangipane tart

makes a 9-inch (23-cm) tart, which serves eight to twelve

This is a coming together. The pastry, frangipane, and streusel can all be
made ahead or close to time and assembled when you're ready to bake. It's a
textural tart, and one that does well with almost any fruit. Berries, though,
are best, especially in summer, but thin slices of stone fruit are also wonderful.

Preheat the oven to 350°F (180°C). Set a 9-inch (23-cm) fluted tart tin with
a removable base onto a baking sheet.

Set the pastry out and onto a floured surface, dusting the top of it lightly
too. With a rolling pin, roll it into a rough circular shape that's about ¼ inch
(6 mm) thick, or a few inches larger than the tin you are using. Carefully
transfer it into the tin, using your fingers to help ease and adjust it in, then
run the pin over the top, to trim off the overhang. Spoon in the frangipane,
slathering it into an even layer, then scatter with the berries, streusel, and
almonds.

Bake for 35 to 45 minutes, until golden brown. Set the tart onto a wire
rack to cool, before lifting it out carefully, coating with sugar, and serving.
It'll keep well, covered at room temperature, for up to 3 days.

PASTRY CRUST (*SEE PAGE 228*)

EXTRA FLOUR FOR THE WORK
SURFACE

FOR THE FILLING

FRANGIPANE (*SEE PAGE 227*)

1 CUP (125 G) RASPBERRIES

FOR THE TOP

STREUSEL (*SEE PAGE 226*)

1 TABLESPOON SLICED
ALMONDS

CONFECTIONERS' SUGAR,
FOR FINISHING

cocoa brownies

Makes about twenty brownies

These were born from a lapse in judgment. They don't need chocolate, instead using only cocoa, which I think gives them an even darker sludge. They're more intense than they seem, and are ideal for standing up to cool, summery things, like berries, crème fraîche, or even ice cream, if you like that contrast sort of thing.

Preheat the oven to 350°F (180°C). Grease and line an 8-inch (20 cm) square baking pan with parchment paper, leaving a slight overhang on the sides.

Put the butter, sugar, cocoa, and salt in a large heatproof bowl, setting it over a saucepan of barely simmering water. Do not let the base of the bowl touch the water below. Heat, stirring often, on medium-low until the mixture is hot and shiny, about 6 minutes. It'll seem a bit dry at first, and won't end up smooth, but thick and almost pastelike. If you have a candy thermometer, it should read at about 250°F (120°C).

Remove the bowl from the pan of water. Whisk in the eggs, one at a time, until smooth, then whisk in the vanilla. Sift the flour over the mixture, then with a large spatula, fold until just combined. The mixture should be thick, sticky, and flowing, like lava. Scrape into the prepared pan, smoothing into an even layer.

Bake for about 20 minutes, until just set, with a slight squidge to it. A skewer inserted into the middle should not come out clean but with damp crumbs attached to it. Let cool in the pan for about 15 minutes, before lifting out and onto a wire rack to cool further. Use a sharp knife to slice them into your desired size, then serve.

¾ CUP (1½ STICKS; 170 G) UNSALTED BUTTER, *PLUS EXTRA FOR GREASING THE PAN*

1½ CUPS (300 G) GRANULATED SUGAR

¾ CUP + 2½ TABLESPOONS (90 G) DUTCH PROCESSED COCOA POWDER

½ TEASPOON SALT

3 LARGE EGGS, *COLD*

1 TABLESPOON VANILLA EXTRACT

⅓ CUP + 2 TABLESPOONS (60 G) ALL-PURPOSE FLOUR

marquise

serves eight

This, perhaps, is one of the chocolatiest desserts I know. It has traits of mousse, ganache, and terrine, but is an entire thing on its own—rich, silky, aerated, yet dense, and very, very decadent. It isn't too sweet, though, but that does depend on the chocolate used. A dark, almost bitter kind is best. Serve with tart berries, or crème fraîche, to cut through the richness.

Line an 8 x 4 x 3-inch (21 x 11 x 7-cm) loaf pan with two layers of plastic wrap, leaving a slight overhang on both sides.

In the bowl of a stand mixer fitted with the whisk attachment, whip the cream to soft and stable peaks on medium speed, then set in the refrigerator to chill until needed.

Put the chocolate and butter into a medium-size heatproof bowl set over a saucepan of barely simmering water on medium-low heat. Do not allow the base of the bowl to touch the water below. Heat, stirring often, until melted, then remove. Whisk in the egg yolks, one at a time, until combined, then sift in the cocoa and salt. Whisk until smooth and thick.

In a separate bowl of a stand mixer, whisk the egg whites on medium speed until foamy. Add in the sugar, a tablespoon at a time, until it is all used up, then turn the speed to high and whisk until a shiny-soft meringue has formed, a few more minutes.

Fold a third of the meringue into the chocolate mixture until streaky, then fold in another third, followed by the last, until almost combined. Add in the whipped cream, and fold, softly, until incorporated. You want the mixture to retain as much aeration as possible, so be careful to not overmix. Scrape into the prepared pan, smoothing it into an even layer. Chill until firm, at least 8 hours, but preferably, overnight.

When you're ready to serve, use the plastic overhang to help lift the marquise out, then cut it into thick slices. It'll be soft, so use a warm and sharp knife, along with decisive cuts, to help slice it. You can also put it into the freezer for a few minutes to help firm it up too.

1 CUP (240 ML) HEAVY CREAM

1¾ CUPS (300 G) FINELY CHOPPED DARK CHOCOLATE

⅔ CUP (1¼ STICKS + 1 TEASPOON; 150 G) UNSALTED BUTTER

4 LARGE EGGS, SEPARATED

¼ CUP (25 G) DUTCH PROCESSED COCOA POWDER

¼ TEASPOON SALT

½ CUP (100 G) GRANULATED SUGAR

tayberry granita

Serves four to six

The lovechild of a raspberry and blackberry, the tayberry is one of the most ravishing fruits. They're plumper, sweeter, and, I find, more perfumed than their parents, belonging to the Rosaceae family, like apples, cherries, roses, and strawberries. They can be hard to find, precious, in fact, and because of that, I don't like to treat them too much. If you can't get them, a mix of raspberries and blackberries, along with a drop of rosewater, will get you close.

Put the tayberries into a food processor or blender and process to form a fine purée.

Next, put the water and sugar into a large saucepan and bring to a boil over medium heat, stirring often, to dissolve the sugar. Remove and allow the syrup to cool, before stirring in the berries and lemon juice. Pour into a shallow dish.

Freeze for about 2 hours, until it has just begun to set around the edges. The time it takes will vary depending on the dish you're using, so keep an eye on it. Stir with a fork, breaking up the ice into crystals and pushing them into the middle, then return to the freezer to set again. Continue to stir every hour or so, until it has transformed into large clumps, about 5 hours total.

When you're ready to serve, fluff it up again, then pile into small bowls.

3½ CUPS + 1 TABLESPOON (450 G) TAYBERRIES

1¼ CUPS + 2 TABLESPOONS (330 ML) WATER

¾ CUP + 2 TABLESPOONS (175 G) GRANULATED SUGAR

2 TABLESPOONS LEMON JUICE

strawberry sumac buckle

makes a 9-inch (23-cm) cake, which serves eight to twelve

Sumac is one of my favorite spices to use, especially with berries, but in particular strawberries. Both are fruity, floral, seductive, and spicy too. You'll sense it in this cake, though it's not too pronounced. There are times that spices should be loud; this isn't one of them. Subtlety is key.

Preheat the oven to 350°F (180°C). Grease and line a 9-inch (23-cm) round cake pan with parchment paper.

First, make the crumb. Combine the sugar, flour, and ground almonds in a bowl. Add in the butter and use your fingers to rub it into the dry ingredients until pea-size clumps have formed. Stir in the chopped almonds, then set aside until needed.

For the cake, whisk together the flour, almonds, sumac, baking powder, baking soda, and salt. Put the butter and sugar into the bowl of a stand mixer fitted with the paddle attachment. Beat, on medium speed, until pale and fluffy, 3 to 5 minutes. Pause mixing to scrape down the bottom and side of the bowl. Add in the eggs, one at a time, beating well to incorporate each addition, then beat in the vanilla extract and orange zest. Lower the speed and add in half the dry ingredients. Beat until just combined, then beat in all the sour cream, followed by the remainder of the dry ingredients, until light, aerated, and well combined. Fold in the strawberries. Scrape into the prepared pan, cover evenly with the crumb, and sprinkle over a pinch of raw sugar.

Bake for 50 to 55 minutes, until golden brown. A skewer inserted into the middle should come out clean. Let the cake cool in the pan for about 15 minutes, then transfer it out and onto a wire rack to cool completely, before dusting with confectioners' sugar and serving.

FOR THE CRUMB

½ CUP (100 G) GRANULATED SUGAR

½ CUP (65 G) ALL-PURPOSE FLOUR

¼ CUP (25 G) GROUND ALMONDS

¼ CUP (½ STICK; 60 G) UNSALTED BUTTER, *COLD AND CUT INTO 1-INCH (2.5-CM) CUBES*

½ CUP (60 G) CHOPPED BLANCHED ALMONDS

FOR THE CAKE

½ CUP (1 STICK; 115 G) UNSALTED BUTTER, *SOFTENED AT ROOM TEMPERATURE, PLUS EXTRA FOR GREASING THE PAN*

2 CUPS (250 G) ALL-PURPOSE FLOUR

½ CUP (50 G) GROUND ALMONDS

1 TEASPOON GROUND SUMAC

1¼ TEASPOONS BAKING POWDER

½ TEASPOON BAKING SODA

¼ TEASPOON SALT

1 CUP (200 G) GRANULATED SUGAR

2 LARGE EGGS

1 TEASPOON VANILLA EXTRACT

ZEST OF AN ORANGE

⅔ CUP (160 ML) SOUR CREAM

1 CUP (200 G) HALVED STRAWBERRIES, *HULLED*

RAW SUGAR, *FOR THE TOP*

CONFECTIONERS' SUGAR, *FOR FINISHING*

ORCHARD

"I've tried to get you out of my head but I can't seem to get you out of my flesh."

—JEANETTE WINTERSON, *Written on the Body*

THE END OF SUMMER. Lessons on how to undo what the body once wanted. The heart, bruised like fallen fruit; once sweet, but with each passing moment, a little more spoiled and rotten. This is the one that hurts the most. It's an end, a departure, and I've never been good at those. But it's also a beginning. Something new is about to unfold, and that's exciting, even if it aches.

Orchard is dedicated to the confrontation between summer and autumn, where things once born from the heat, taint, toward the cool. It's, in one word, ripe. A glut of fruit, soft, fallen, and sunken, heavy to be held. The weather is confused. Warm on some days, but stormed on others, with the first chill beginning to set in. And that's okay. The seasons should never happen like clockwork, but bleed, wild, with desire.

The change in the air is reflected on the table. How we cook has begun to warm, shifting in preparation for the darker months ahead. It's not about perfection, but instead, for taking things in their natural state—even the damaged ones. There's more spice, earthiness, and comfort. And it's pregnant. We live for the new but we're not yet done with the old. Or rather, it's not done with us.

The time, as muddled as the air that surrounds, in many ways bittersweet, but brilliant, nonetheless.

late summer cake

makes an 8 x 4-inch (21 x 11-cm) loaf, which serves eight to ten

This is a fleshy cake. It's made with a large amount of almonds that keep
it soft, along with a studding of fruit that serves to keep it moist and damp.
It's adaptable too. You can play around with what fruit you use for it. I like
peaches and raspberries, or blueberries and apricot, but I imagine that
plum would be wonderful too, even cherry.

Preheat the oven to 350°F (180°C). Grease and line an 8 x 4 x 3-inch
(21 x 11 x 7-cm) loaf pan with parchment paper, leaving a slight overhang
on both sides.

Whisk together the almonds, flour, baking powder, cinnamon, and salt.

In the bowl of a stand mixer fitted with the paddle attachment, beat the
butter and both sugars on medium speed until light and fluffy, 3 to 5 minutes.
Pause to scrape down the bottom and side of the bowl. Add the eggs, one
at a time, beating well to incorporate each addition, then mix in the vanilla
and orange zest. Lower the speed and tip in the dry ingredients. Beat until
a soft and aerated batter has formed, no more than a few minutes. Fold
in the fruits. Scrape into the prepared pan, using an offset palette knife to
smooth it out, then scatter with a handful of streusel.

Bake for about an hour, until golden brown. A skewer inserted into the
middle should not come out clean, but with a few moist crumbs attached
to it. Let cool in the pan for 15 minutes before lifting it out and onto a wire
rack to cool further. Dust with confectioners' sugar to finish.

¾ CUP + 2 TABLESPOONS
(1½ STICKS + 2 TABLESPOONS;
200 G) UNSALTED BUTTER,
*SOFTENED AT ROOM
TEMPERATURE, PLUS EXTRA
FOR GREASING THE PAN*

1½ CUPS (145 G) GROUND
ALMONDS

½ CUP (65 G) ALL-PURPOSE
FLOUR

1¼ TEASPOONS BAKING
POWDER

1 TEASPOON GROUND
CINNAMON

½ TEASPOON SALT

¾ CUP + 1 TABLESPOON (165 G)
GRANULATED SUGAR

¼ CUP (55 G) LIGHT BROWN
SUGAR

3 LARGE EGGS

1 TEASPOON VANILLA EXTRACT

ZEST OF ½ ORANGE

1 CUP (125 G) BERRIES
(*BLACKBERRIES, RASPBERRIES,
BOYSENBERRIES, OR
BLACKCURRANTS*)

1 CUP (200 G) SLICED STONE
FRUIT (*APRICOTS, PEACHES,
PLUMS, CHERRIES, OR
NECTARINES) IN ¼-INCH
(6-MM) PIECES*

STREUSEL (*SEE PAGE 226*)

CONFECTIONERS' SUGAR,
FOR FINISHING

pêche de vigne sorbet

serves four to six

Pêche de vigne, or vine peaches, are elusive. They don't appear often, but when they do, it's for a short while, often the last few weeks of the season. A cross between a peach and a plum, their taste is unlike anything else— sweet, perfumed, and when you get a good one, bloody. Because of how brief their span is, I've come to freezing them when I see them, or purchasing them in puréed form, a salve for this sorbet. You could use other stone fruits as a replacement, like plums, even mixing them with peaches, for something similar, but keep a lookout. You'll know why once you taste it.

Pour the pêche de vigne into a large bowl and set it aside but near the space where you'll be working.

Put the sugar, water, lemon peel, lemon juice, and cloves into a medium-size saucepan set over medium-low heat. Cook, stirring often, until the sugar has dissolved, then raise the heat and let the mixture come to a simmer. Remove and pour into the fruit, discarding the lemon peel. Stir until combined, then stir in the vodka, if using. Cover and set in the refrigerator to chill until cold, at least 8 hours, but preferably overnight.

Transfer the mixture into an ice cream machine and churn according to the manufacturer's instructions. It will be thick and near doubled in size when it's done. Scrape into a container, cover, and freeze until just firm before serving.

2 POUNDS (906 G) PÊCHE DE VIGNE, *PURÉED*

¾ CUP + 2 TABLESPOONS (175 G) GRANULATED SUGAR

¾ CUP (180 ML) WATER

A THICK STRIP OF LEMON PEEL

JUICE OF A LEMON

A PINCH OF GROUND CLOVES

3 TABLESPOONS VODKA, *OPTIONAL*

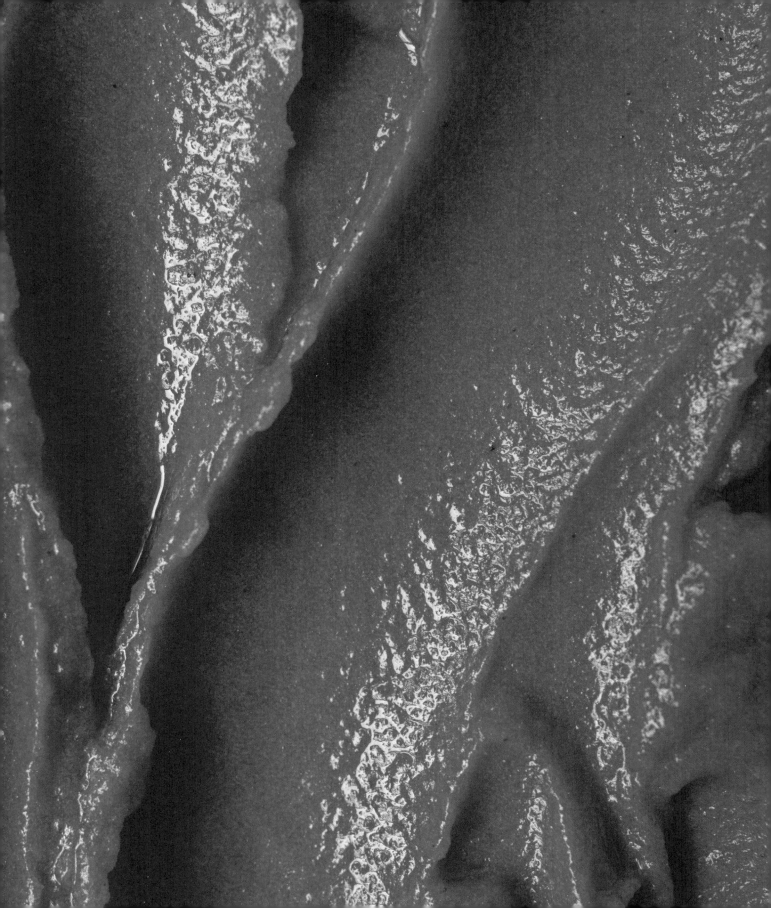

plum and hazelnut financiers

makes twelve financiers

I make these often in an effort to use up all the extra egg whites from the ice cream I churn. They're laden with hazelnuts, studded with fruit, and warm from an undertone of spice too. You could use any kind you'd like, but I think plums are best. They have a brood that matches the cake perfectly.

Preheat the oven to 350°F (180°C). Lightly grease a twelve-cup financier mold or muffin pan with a little extra butter.

Put the butter into a deep saucepan. Heat, stirring often, until golden and melted. Turn the heat to medium-high and continue to cook, swirling often but not stirring, until a deep-amber-hued liquid has formed. It will foam, hiss, and crackle but should subside as it nears done. Set aside to cool.

Meanwhile, whisk together the hazelnuts, flour, cloves, and salt in a large mixing bowl, then stir in the sugar. Give the egg whites a light whisk in a small bowl to loosen them up, then add them to the dry ingredients. Whisk until just incorporated. Stream in the browned butter, whisking as you go, until smooth. Mix in the brandy, if using. Spoon the batter into the molds, filling them no more than two-thirds full, then top each with a few slices of plum.

Bake for 20 to 25 minutes, until golden brown. Let cool in the pan slightly, then run a blunt knife around their edges, easing the financiers out and onto a wire rack to cool further. Dust with confectioners' sugar before serving. They're best eaten soon after making but will keep well for a few days stored in an airtight container at room temperature.

½ CUP (1 STICK; 115 G) UNSALTED BUTTER, *PLUS EXTRA FOR GREASING THE MOLD*

2¾ CUPS (265 G) GROUND HAZELNUTS

½ CUP (65 G) ALL-PURPOSE FLOUR

A PINCH OF GROUND CLOVES

½ TEASPOON SALT

1½ CUPS (300 G) GRANULATED SUGAR

5 LARGE EGG WHITES

1 TABLESPOON BRANDY, *OPTIONAL*

4 MEDIUM DARK PLUMS, *CUT INTO SLICES*

CONFECTIONERS' SUGAR, *FOR FINISHING*

red fruit crumble

serves four

Crumble is one of the simplest things but also one of the most temperamental. The amount of sugar needed will rest on how sweet your fruit is: too much and it'll overwhelm; too little and it'll pale, so alter as you see fit. It should be paired with ice cream too. There's nothing like a collision between hot and cold, and there's a good vanilla in this book (*see page 62*).

Preheat the oven to 350°F (180°C).

Tear up the almond paste and put it into a food processor. Add the butter, vanilla, almond extract, and salt. Process until a smooth and creamy paste has formed, pausing as needed to scrape down the bottom and side of the bowl. Scrape into a mixing bowl, then add the flour, oats, ground almonds, sugar, and zest. Use your fingers to rub it all together until rough pebble-sized clumps have formed. Toss through the shaved almonds.

To prepare the fruit, in a separate bowl, combine the plums, raspberries, sugar, and amaretto, if using. Toss until the fruit is coated, then tip into a 2-quart (2-L) deep baking dish. Pile the crumble over the top.

Bake for about an hour, until golden brown. The juices should be sticky and seeped, and the plums tender, but not to the point of disintegration. Allow to cool before serving warm soon after.

FOR THE CRUMBLE

²/₃ CUP (175 G) ALMOND PASTE
(*SEE PAGE 223*)

½ CUP (1 STICK; 115 G)
UNSALTED BUTTER, *SOFTENED
AT ROOM TEMPERATURE*

1 TEASPOON VANILLA EXTRACT

½ TEASPOON ALMOND EXTRACT

½ TEASPOON SALT

1 CUP (125 G) ALL-PURPOSE
FLOUR

²/₃ CUP (50 G) ROLLED OATS

¼ CUP + 2 TEASPOONS (30 G)
GROUND ALMONDS

¼ CUP (50 G) GRANULATED
SUGAR

ZEST OF AN ORANGE

¼ CUP (30 G) SHAVED ALMONDS

FOR THE FRUIT

ABOUT 6 MEDIUM PLUMS (400 G),
PEELED AND HALVED

2 CUPS RASPBERRIES (250 G)

¼ CUP + 2 TABLESPOONS (75 G)
GRANULATED SUGAR

2 TABLESPOONS AMARETTO,
OPTIONAL

dacquoise

serves six to eight

When a plum is so beautiful in its natural state, it's a shame to do too much. Dacquoise is the perfect thing to highlight it. It's made up of layers of meringue, fruit, and cream, and it is as messy as you can imagine. But that's all part of the charm. There's something about the heat that makes me want to live with less refinement—dirtier, and ripe. It shows.

Preheat the oven to 350°F (180°C). Lightly oil and line a 12 x 9 x 1-inch (30 x 22 x 2.5-cm) jelly-roll pan with parchment paper. To prepare the meringue, spread the walnuts onto a separate baking sheet. Roast for 10 to 12 minutes, until golden brown, then remove and let cool before chopping into small chunks. Lower the temperature to 300°F (150°C).

In the bowl of a stand mixer fitted with the whisk attachment, whisk the egg whites and salt on medium speed until soft and foamy. Add the sugar, a tablespoon at a time, until it is all used up. Turn the speed to high. Continue to whisk for a few more minutes, until thick and glossy, then fold in the walnuts. Scrape into the prepared pan, using an offset palette knife to smooth it into an even layer.

Bake for 25 to 30 minutes, until light brown, puffed, and cracked. Transfer to a wire rack to cool completely before assembling.

Meanwhile, to make the filling, in the bowl of a stand mixer fitted with the whisk attachment, whisk the cream, crème fraîche, sugar, vanilla seeds, and brandy, if using, until soft but stable peaks have formed. Transfer to the refrigerator to keep cold until needed.

Once the meringue has cooled, carefully lift it out, then use a sharp knife to cut it into even-size thirds from the longest edge. Put the first piece on a serving plate, spread over half the cream, then scatter with half the plum slices. Lay on the next piece of meringue, using a light touch to press it into the filling below, then cover with the remaining cream and plums. Top with the final piece of meringue.

Chill to firm up slightly, then dust with confectioners' sugar before serving. It's best eaten soon after.

FOR THE MERINGUE

NEUTRAL OIL FOR PREPARING THE PAN

1¼ CUPS (180 G) WALNUTS

4 LARGE EGG WHITES

A PINCH OF SALT

1 CUP + 3½ TABLESPOONS (240 G) GRANULATED SUGAR

FOR THE FILLING

1 CUP (240 ML) HEAVY CREAM

¼ CUP (60 G) CRÈME FRAÎCHE *(SEE PAGE 225)*

3 TABLESPOONS GRANULATED SUGAR

SEEDS OF A VANILLA BEAN

1 TABLESPOON BRANDY, *OPTIONAL*

1 LARGE PLUM, *PITTED AND THINLY SLICED*

CONFECTIONERS' SUGAR, *FOR FINISHING*

dark chocolate cremeux

serves four

This is one of the dreamiest custards ever. It's not too sweet, but it is rich, and I find that it needs something bright to cut through how intense it is, like an apricot or plum. It is all about the chocolate, though, so use the best you can find. A bitter, dark kind is best.

Put the chocolate into a large bowl, setting it aside but near the space where you'll be working.

Pour the milk and cream into a medium-size saucepan. Heat, over medium-low, until it reaches a simmer. Meanwhile, whisk the yolks and sugar until pale and fluffy in a heatproof bowl. It should be thick and almost nearing ribbon stage, holding a trail that flows back onto itself when the whisk is lifted.

Slip a little stream of the hot milk mixture into the yolks, whisking well to acclimatize them to the heat, then pour it all into the saucepan set on the stove. Continue to cook, stirring constantly and concentrating the action around the edges of the pan, until it is thick enough to coat the back of a spoon. Remove and pour over the chocolate, whisking until smooth, then stir in the brandy, if using. Cover with plastic wrap, pressing it onto the surface to prevent a skin from forming. Chill overnight.

When you're ready to serve, spoon the cremeux into bowls and serve alongside thin slices of stone fruit. It will keep, cold, for up to 3 days.

1 CUP + 1 TABLESPOON (180 G) FINELY CHOPPED DARK CHOCOLATE

1 CUP (240 ML) WHOLE MILK

⅔ CUP (160 ML) HEAVY CREAM

4 LARGE EGG YOLKS

¼ CUP + 2 TABLESPOONS (75 G) GRANULATED SUGAR

1 TABLESPOON BRANDY, *OPTIONAL*

STONE FRUIT (*APRICOTS, CHERRIES, PEACHES, OR PLUMS*), *THINLY SLICED FOR SERVING*

black forest cookies

makes twenty to twenty-four cookies

I never thought I would like double chocolate cookies as much as I do until I met these. They're dark, decadent, and dressed in the flavors of a classic black forest—cherry, chocolate, and sometimes, espresso. If you can't find sour cherries you could use cranberries instead. It won't be true to the real thing, but then again, these aren't either. It'll come close.

Whisk together the flour, cocoa, espresso, baking soda, and salt.

In the bowl of a stand mixer fitted with the paddle attachment, beat the butter and sugar on medium speed until light and fluffy, 3 to 5 minutes. Pause to scrape down the bottom and side of the bowl. Add the eggs, one at a time, beating well to incorporate each addition, then beat in the vanilla. Set the speed to low and tip in the dry ingredients. Beat until a soft dough has begun to form, then mix in the chocolate and cherries. Chill until firm, half an hour.

Meanwhile, set oven racks in the lower and upper thirds of the oven. Preheat to 350°F (180°C). Line two large baking sheets with parchment paper.

Using a cookie scoop or generous tablespoon as a measure, scoop the dough into even portions. If you're using a spoon, roll them into balls. Divide between the prepared sheets, placing them a few inches apart to allow for spreading. You should be able to fit 8 to 10 per sheet. Keep the leftover dough balls in the refrigerator to be baked off later, or store in the freezer for up to 2 months. Sprinkle flaked salt over the tops.

Bake for 10 to 12 minutes, rotating the sheets top to bottom and bottom to top halfway through, until the cookies are puffed and the edges crisp. Let the cookies stand on the sheets for a few minutes before transferring them off and onto a wire rack to cool further, before serving.

1¾ CUPS + 2 TABLESPOONS (235 G) ALL-PURPOSE FLOUR

½ CUP + 3 TABLESPOONS (65 G) DUTCH PROCESSED COCOA POWDER

2 TEASPOONS ESPRESSO POWDER

1 TEASPOON BAKING SODA

½ TEASPOON SALT

¾ CUP + 2 TABLESPOONS (1½ STICKS + 2 TABLESPOONS; 200 G) UNSALTED BUTTER, *SOFTENED AT ROOM TEMPERATURE*

1 CUP (200 G) GRANULATED SUGAR

2 LARGE EGGS

1 TABLESPOON VANILLA EXTRACT

¾ CUP + 1 TABLESPOON (140 G) COARSELY CHOPPED DARK CHOCOLATE

½ CUP + 1 TABLESPOON (75 G) CHOPPED DRIED SOUR CHERRIES

FLAKED SALT, *FOR FINISHING*

fig clove fregolotta

makes a 13-inch (33-cm) tart, which serves eight

This Italian dessert lands somewhere among a biscuit, a tart, and a crumble, made up of a shortbread-like dough that's used as both base and top, then filled with jam. It's meant to be rustic, rough, and broken. There's beauty in that.

Preheat the oven to 350°F (180°C). Set a 13 x 4-inch (33 x 10-cm) fluted tart tin with a removable base on a baking sheet.

Put the flour, ground hazelnuts, polenta, sugar, cloves, salt, and zest in the bowl of a food processor. Process to distribute the ingredients. Toss in the butter. Pulse until just incorporated, with some larger chunks of it running throughout. Add the egg yolks and pulse again until a soft, crumble-like dough has formed, no more than 20 seconds. It should be moist, clumpy, and able to hold itself when pinched together.

Tip three-quarters of the dough into the tin and use your fingers to press it into an even layer. Spoon over the jam then crumble on the remaining dough. Scatter the chopped hazelnuts over the crumble.

Bake for 25 to 30 minutes, until golden brown. Transfer to a wire rack to cool at room temperature, then unmold, carefully. It'll be quite tender, so take care. Dust with a flourish of confectioners' sugar before serving.

1¼ CUPS + 1 TEASPOON (160 G) ALL-PURPOSE FLOUR

1¼ CUPS (120 G) GROUND HAZELNUTS

¼ CUP (40 G) POLENTA

½ CUP + 1 TABLESPOON (115 G) GRANULATED SUGAR

A PINCH OF GROUND CLOVES

¼ TEASPOON SALT

ZEST OF ½ ORANGE

¾ CUP + 2 TABLESPOONS (1½ STICKS + 2 TABLESPOONS; 200 G) UNSALTED BUTTER, *COLD AND CUT INTO ½-INCH (12-MM) CUBES*

2 LARGE EGG YOLKS

⅔ CUP (215 G) FIG JAM

1 TABLESPOON CHOPPED HAZELNUTS

CONFECTIONERS' SUGAR, *FOR FINISHING*

mulled wine ice cream

serves four to six

This is the kind of thing that shouldn't make sense, but does. It's a contradiction, almost—soft but strong, cool but warm, and bittersweet. There's a lot of cream in it too, more than in most ice creams, which makes it very potent and meant for ending.

First, mull the wine. Pour the wine into a medium-size saucepan, then stir in the cinnamon, juniper, star anise, cloves, nutmeg, orange peel, and sugar. Bring the mixture to a slow boil over medium heat, then remove from heat and steep for 30 minutes.

To make the ice cream, pour the cream and milk into a large saucepan. Place a fine-mesh sieve over it, then stream through the mulled wine, using the back of a spoon to press on the spices to help release any infused juices, then discard them. Bring to a simmer over medium-low heat. Meanwhile, whisk the yolks and sugar until pale and thick in a medium-size heatproof bowl.

Slip a little stream of the hot cream into the yolks, whisking constantly to acclimatize them to the heat, then pour it all back into the saucepan set on the stove. Continue to cook, stirring constantly, until it is thick enough to coat the back of a spoon. It shouldn't take more than a few minutes. Remove from the heat and stir in the bitters, if using. Strain into a bowl, then cover with plastic wrap, pressing it onto the surface of the custard to prevent a skin from forming. Chill until cold, at least 8 hours but preferably overnight.

Transfer to an ice cream machine and churn according to the manufacturer's instructions. It'll be at an almost soft-serve–like consistency when it's done. Scrape into a container, cover, and freeze until just firm, before serving.

FOR THE MULLED WINE

1 CUP (240 ML) RED WINE

1 CINNAMON STICK

3 DRIED JUNIPER BERRIES

2 WHOLE STAR ANISE

¼ TEASPOON GROUND CLOVES

A PINCH OF GRATED NUTMEG

A THICK STRIP OF ORANGE PEEL

¼ CUP (50 G) GRANULATED SUGAR

FOR THE ICE CREAM

2 CUPS (480 ML) HEAVY CREAM

¼ CUP (60 ML) WHOLE MILK

5 LARGE EGG YOLKS

½ CUP (100 G) GRANULATED SUGAR

DASH OF ANGOSTURA BITTERS, *OPTIONAL*

drunken fig brownies

makes twelve to sixteen brownies

I would go as far as to say that these are the most indulgent brownies, ever. They're rich with chocolate, wine, and fig, and have an interior that's almost similar to ganache. You'll wonder if they'll ever set, and sometimes, I think, that's how brownies should be—undone.

Preheat the oven to 350°F (180°C). Grease and line an 8-inch (20-cm) square baking pan with parchment paper, leaving a slight overhang on the sides.

Chop the figs into rough chunks, then toss them into a medium saucepan and tip in the port. Give the pan a gentle shake to nudge them into the port. There won't be enough of it to cover; rather, it'll just get their feet wet. Bring the mixture to a simmer, then turn off the heat and cover the pan, setting it aside to give the figs time to soften.

Next, sift together the flour, cocoa, baking powder, and salt. Put the chocolate and butter into a medium-size heatproof bowl set over a saucepan filled with a few inches of barely simmering water. Do not let the base of the bowl touch the water below. Cook, stirring often, until melted. Remove and pour into a large bowl, adding both sugars, and whisking until combined. Add the eggs, one at a time, whisking to incorporate each addition, then whisk in the vanilla. It should be smooth and glossy.

Tip in the dry ingredients and fold until almost combined, then pour in all of the fig mixture. Fold until incorporated. Scrape into the prepared pan, smoothing it into an even layer.

Bake for 25 to 35 minutes, until the edges are firm and the middle just set. Transfer to a wire rack and let cool in the pan. It'll be tempting to unmold early, but do your best to refrain. It needs time to settle. Let it.

When you're ready to serve, use the overhanging parchment to lift the brownie out. Dust the top of it with a good amount of cocoa powder, then cut into small squares. They'll keep well, covered and stored in an airtight container for up to 3 days.

FOR THE FIGS

1 CUP (150 G) DRIED FIGS

⅓ CUP (80 ML) PORT

FOR THE BROWNIES

⅔ CUP (1¼ STICKS + 1 TEASPOON; 150 G) UNSALTED BUTTER, *PLUS EXTRA FOR GREASING THE PAN*

1 CUP (125 G) ALL-PURPOSE FLOUR

1 CUP + 1 TABLESPOON (90 G) DUTCH PROCESSED COCOA POWDER

½ TEASPOON BAKING POWDER

1 TEASPOON SALT

2 CUPS (340 G) FINELY CHOPPED DARK CHOCOLATE

1 CUP + 2 TABLESPOONS (225 G) GRANULATED SUGAR

¾ CUP + 2 TEASPOONS (175 G) LIGHT BROWN SUGAR

4 LARGE EGGS, *COLD*

1 TABLESPOON VANILLA EXTRACT

DUTCH PROCESSED COCOA POWDER, *FOR FINISHING*

tart cherry semifreddo

serves eight

The cold does it for me, and this is one of the things that I'll always run to.
It's tart, but sweet, with a texture that's rather unbelievable—rich, silky, and
aerated, like mousse, but also like ice cream, and almost indescribable. The
hardest part is waiting for it to freeze, so plan ahead, as it needs time.

Line an 8 x 4 x 3-inch (21 x 11 x 7-cm) loaf pan with two layers of plastic
wrap, leaving a slight overhang on both sides.

To make the purée, put the cherries, sugar, kirsch, lemon zest, and lemon
juice into a medium-size saucepan over medium heat. Give it a stir, then
heat until the sugar has dissolved. Continue to cook until the fruit has
softened, about 6 minutes. It should be syrupy too. Remove and transfer
to a blender, and blend to form a smooth purée. A few larger chunks of
cherry are fine to remain if you'd like. Leave to cool.

Next make the semifreddo. In the bowl of a stand mixer fitted with the
whisk attachment, whisk the cream, crème fraîche, and vanilla to the point
of soft peaks. Keep cold in the refrigerator until needed.

Put the eggs and sugar into the bowl of a stand mixer and set it over a
saucepan filled with a few inches of barely simmering water. Do not let the
base of the bowl touch the water below. Heat, stirring often, slowly, until it
reaches 170°F (75°C) on a candy thermometer. Remove the bowl and set it
onto the stand mixer fitted with the whisk attachment. Whisk on high speed
until pale, thick, and doubled in volume, 6 to 8 minutes. It should leave a
trail that flows onto itself when the whisk is lifted, and the bowl should no
longer be hot to the touch.

Fold half the cream mixture into the egg mixture until almost combined,
then fold in the remaining half. It's fine for some streaks to remain, better in
fact, as you don't want it to lose too much aeration. Add in the purée and
fold until rippled. The less you fold, the more distinct it will be, so do it for
as little as possible. Scrape into the prepared pan. Cover and freeze until
firm before unmolding, slicing, and serving.

FOR THE PURÉE

1¼ CUPS (280 G) CHERRIES,
PITTED

¼ CUP (50 G) GRANULATED
SUGAR

1 TABLESPOON KIRSCH, *OPTIONAL*

ZEST AND JUICE OF A LEMON

FOR THE SEMIFREDDO

1 CUP (240 ML) HEAVY CREAM

¼ CUP (60 G) CRÈME FRAÎCHE
(*SEE PAGE 225*)

1 TABLESPOON VANILLA EXTRACT

4 LARGE EGGS

¾ CUP + 2 TABLESPOONS (175 G)
GRANULATED SUGAR

bostock

makes eight

There's not much else to this other than a few components that need to be put together; nothing, though, that can't be done quickly. The end result is worth it. A nutty, golden, and toasted pastry, somewhat similar to an almond croissant, best served with ripe fruit.

Set oven racks in the lower and upper thirds of the oven. Preheat to 350°F (180°C). Line two large baking sheets with parchment paper.

To make the syrup, put the water, sugar, lemon peel, and brandy, if using, in a small saucepan. Heat, stirring often, until the sugar has dissolved. Set aside to cool.

Next, divide the brioche slices between the prepared sheets, leaving a few inches of space between them. Use a pastry brush to moisten each with a little of the syrup, then slather on a few generous tablespoons of the frangipane, using an offset palette knife to smooth it out almost to the edges. Scatter the almonds over them.

Bake for 20 to 25 minutes, until golden brown. Let cool for a few minutes, before dusting with confectioners' sugar and serving with slices of fruit. They're best eaten warm, soon after making, but leftovers can be kept in an airtight container in the refrigerator. Reheat before serving.

FOR THE SYRUP

⅓ CUP (80 ML) WATER

½ CUP (100 G) GRANULATED SUGAR

A THICK STRIP OF LEMON PEEL

SPLASH OF BRANDY, *OPTIONAL*

8 SLICES BRIOCHE (*SEE PAGE 224*), *CUT ½ INCH (12 MM) THICK*

FRANGIPANE (*SEE PAGE 227*)

⅓ CUP (40 G) SHAVED ALMONDS

CONFECTIONERS' SUGAR, *FOR FINISHING*

SLICED STONE FRUIT (APRICOTS, PEACHES, PLUMS, OR NECTARINES), *FOR SERVING*

oat biscuits
with apricot, rosemary,
and white chocolate

makes eight biscuits

I prefer biscuits to cookies. It's contentious, but there is a difference. A biscuit should have a significant heft in comparison to its fickle and overly sweet counterpart, and be robust too. These are that and more. I like to use white chocolate in them, for the caramelization it develops when baked, but if you aren't a fan of it, a good, dark kind will work too.

Stir together the flour, oats, rosemary, baking powder, and salt.

In the bowl of a stand mixer fitted with the paddle attachment, beat the butter and sugar on medium speed until creamy, 3 minutes. Beat in the vanilla and orange zest. Pause mixing to scrape down the bottom and side of the bowl then turn the speed to low. Tip in the dry ingredients and beat until almost combined. It should still be a bit floury. Mix in the chocolate and apricots. Chill until just firm, 30 minutes.

Meanwhile, set oven racks in the lower and upper thirds of the oven. Preheat to 350°F (180°C). Line two large baking sheets with parchment paper.

Tip the dough out and onto a lightly floured work surface. Use your hands to pat it into a mound about 1 inch (2.5 cm) thick, then use a 2½-inch (6-cm) round cookie cutter to stamp out as many circles as possible from it. Divide the biscuits between the baking sheets, placing them a few inches apart for spreading, then reroll the scraps and repeat. Sprinkle with salt.

Bake for 16 to 18 minutes, rotating the sheets top to bottom and bottom to top halfway through, until light golden brown. Let the biscuits cool on the sheet for a few minutes before transferring them off and onto a wire rack to cool completely. They can be stored in an airtight container at room temperature for up to 5 days.

1¾ CUPS + 1 TABLESPOON (225 G) ALL-PURPOSE FLOUR, *PLUS EXTRA FOR THE WORK SURFACE*

2 CUPS (160 G) ROLLED OATS

1 TABLESPOON CHOPPED ROSEMARY

1 TEASPOON BAKING POWDER

½ TEASPOON SALT

1 CUP (2 STICKS; 230 G) UNSALTED BUTTER, *SOFTENED AT ROOM TEMPERATURE*

¾ CUP + 2 TABLESPOONS (175 G) GRANULATED SUGAR

1 TEASPOON VANILLA EXTRACT

ZEST OF AN ORANGE

¾ CUP + 1 TABLESPOON (140 G) COARSELY CHOPPED WHITE CHOCOLATE

½ CUP (85 G) CHOPPED DRIED APRICOTS

SEA SALT FLAKES, *FOR FINISHING*

white peach and ginger cake

makes an 8-inch (20-cm) cake, which serves eight to twelve

To say this is a soft cake would be an understatement. The crumb has a cloud-fleece quality, sort of like fairy floss, with peaches suspended throughout it. But despite how fragile it is, it holds itself well, for days, in fact. It's bright, but stormed, and wonderful eaten under the late sun, chill on its way.

Preheat the oven to 350°F (180°C). Grease and line an 8-inch (20-cm) round cake pan with parchment paper.

Sift together the flour, almonds, ginger, baking powder, baking soda, and salt.

In the bowl of a stand mixer fitted with the paddle attachment, cream the butter and sugar on medium speed until pale and fluffy, 3 to 5 minutes. Pause mixing to scrape down the bottom and side of the bowl. Add in the eggs, one at a time, beating well to incorporate each addition, then beat in the vanilla. Lower the speed. Beat in half the dry ingredients, followed by all the sour cream, then the last of the dry ingredients, until light and aerated. Fold in the peaches. Scrape into the prepared pan and top with enough streusel to coat.

Bake for 45 to 50 minutes, until light golden brown. A skewer inserted into the middle should come out clean. Let the cake cool in the pan for 15 minutes before transferring it out and onto a wire rack to cool completely. Dust with confectioners' sugar, before serving.

½ CUP (1 STICK; 115 G) UNSALTED BUTTER, *SOFTENED AT ROOM TEMPERATURE, PLUS EXTRA FOR GREASING THE PAN*

1½ CUPS (190 G) ALL-PURPOSE FLOUR

⅔ CUP (65 G) GROUND ALMONDS

1 TEASPOON GROUND GINGER

1¼ TEASPOONS BAKING POWDER

½ TEASPOON BAKING SODA

½ TEASPOON SALT

¾ CUP (150 G) GRANULATED SUGAR

2 LARGE EGGS

1 TEASPOON VANILLA EXTRACT

¾ CUP (180 G) SOUR CREAM

3 WHITE PEACHES, *CHOPPED INTO ROUGH CHUNKS*

STREUSEL, *FOR THE TOP* (*SEE PAGE 226*)

CONFECTIONERS' SUGAR, *FOR FINISHING*

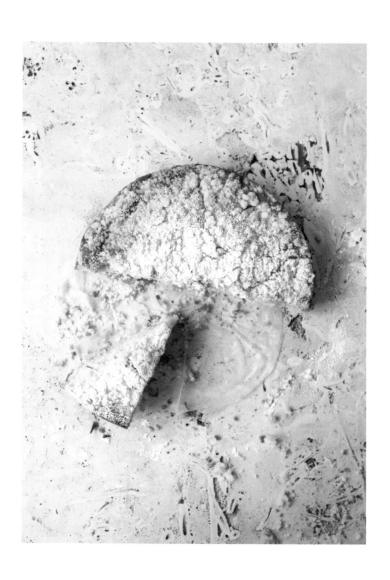

WOODLAND

"It was here in the woods where the woods were caught
in their dying and you held me well."

—ANNE SEXTON, "The Expatriates"

I LOST MYSELF ONCE in a woodland. It wasn't where I intended to be, but rather it was where I was meant to be. I remember it well, for the season was slow that year. The trees were stark, their leaves lost to a ground littered with rust. The air was cold and still, near silent, save for the snap of a twig to remind that inside it, you're never alone. There were no signs of life. It was as if all that existed had met surrender, and as I continued to tread, I too surrendered.

That's what the woodland does best. Wander in and it'll eat you whole, like a wolf. We know that from childhood. It keeps hidden things hid, and in. It'll hold you in too, until it's done. Only then will the path out be made clear. But despite its strength, the wood is vulnerable.

A most beautiful cycle of life, death, and decay, it shows us how important it is to release, shed. And then comes regeneration. The woodland, fertile, even in her dying.

This is a chapter that comes from the ground. It's not clean, but muddied, dirtied, earthen, and smudged. Within, you'll find nuts, seeds, spices, and roots, as well as deep, dark, sugars. All things that furrow. It hides too. Each time I cook from it, I discover something new, that perhaps wasn't ready to come to light before and needed to be trodden on to be felt.

The year has now reached its peak and slowly, we're beginning to turn inward, toward decline. The cold, the gnaw, the end. But hold on, there's more.

truffles

makes about forty truffles

The secret to a good truffle rests in the ganache. It should be intense and smooth, with a texture that melts. I like to use the barest amount of clove in mine, which gives it this carnal grit. It is all about the chocolate, though, so please use the best you can find.

Put the chocolate into a large bowl. Set it aside but near the space where you'll be working.

Combine the cream and crème fraîche in a medium saucepan. Heat, over medium-low, until it comes to a simmer, then pour it over the chocolate. Let the mixture stand for a minute to acclimatize, then whisk until smooth. Whisk in the cloves and salt. Scrape into a container and transfer to the refrigerator to chill until firm, about 4 hours.

To finish, put the cocoa powder in a shallow bowl for coating. With a just-warmed teaspoon, scoop out balls from the ganache, rattling each in the powder, until coated. You can be as rough or as refined as you'd like in their shaping. It's all good. Keep cold in the refrigerator before serving. They'll store for about one week.

2 CUPS (340 G) FINELY CHOPPED DARK CHOCOLATE

1 ¼ CUPS (300 ML) HEAVY CREAM

2 ½ TABLESPOONS CRÈME FRAÎCHE (*SEE PAGE 225*)

¼ TEASPOON GROUND CLOVES

A PINCH OF SALT

DUTCH PROCESSED COCOA POWDER, *FOR COATING*

beetroot mud cake

makes a 9-inch cake (23-cm), which serves eight to twelve

If the beetroot fools you into thinking this is something good, think again. Strong, it turns the cake earthy, dirty, and dense, sludgelike too. It's called mud cake for a reason. I think beetroot and chocolate are one of the best combinations. When paired, they come to life, and need each other to function, like soul mates. And I'm glad to let them meet. Perhaps there's good in it after all.

Preheat the oven to 350°F (180°C). Grease and line a 9-inch (23-cm) round springform cake pan with parchment paper.

Put the butter and chocolate in a medium-size heatproof bowl set over a saucepan filled with a few inches of barely simmering water. Do not let the base of the bowl touch the water below. Heat, stirring often, until melted, then remove and stir in the brandy. Whisk in ⅔ cup (135 g) of the sugar, then whisk in the yolks, one at a time, until glossy. Mix in the beetroot.

Next, put the egg whites into the bowl of a stand mixer fitted with the whisk attachment. Whisk, on medium-high speed, until foamy, then scatter in the remaining sugar, whisking to firm peaks. Fold half into the chocolate mixture to loosen, then fold in the remaining half, until just incorporated. A fair few marbled streaks should remain. Sift in the flour, cocoa powder, baking powder, and salt, then again fold until a uniform batter has formed. Scrape into the prepared pan.

Bake for 30 to 35 minutes, until crackled. A skewer inserted into the middle should come out almost clean, with a few dense crumbs attached to it. Let cool in the pan for 15 minutes before lifting it out and onto a wire rack to cool completely. Finish with a good dusting of cocoa powder.

⅔ CUP (1¼ STICKS + 1 TEASPOON; 150 G) UNSALTED BUTTER, *PLUS EXTRA FOR GREASING THE PAN*

1¼ CUPS (215 G) FINELY CHOPPED DARK CHOCOLATE

2 TABLESPOONS BRANDY

¾ CUP + 2 TABLESPOONS (175 G) GRANULATED SUGAR

3 LARGE EGGS, *SEPARATED*

3 CUPS (250 G) FINELY GRATED FRESH BEETROOT

¾ CUP + 1 TABLESPOON (100 G) ALL-PURPOSE FLOUR

¼ CUP (25 G) DUTCH PROCESSED COCOA POWDER, *PLUS EXTRA FOR FINISHING*

¾ TEASPOON BAKING POWDER

½ TEASPOON SALT

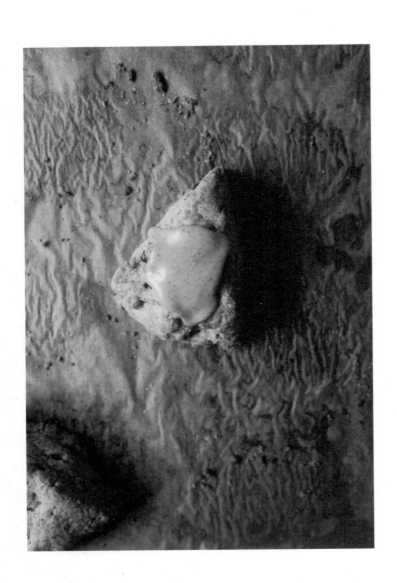

pecan scones

makes eight scones

These aren't the kind for splitting and slathering. Rather, they're dessert scones—sweet and rich, studded with pecans, and glazed. That's the part I like best. It has a stickiness that not only coats but seeps right down into the crumb. Be sure to eat them soon after making, warm.

Set oven racks in the lower and upper thirds of the oven. Preheat to 350°F (180°C). First, make the scones. Line two large baking sheets with parchment paper. Scatter the pecans on one of the sheets and roast until golden brown, 10 to 12 minutes. Set aside to cool.

Next, whisk the flour, baking powder, cinnamon, salt, and sugar in a large mixing bowl. Add the butter cubes and toss to coat. With a pastry blender or a metal spatula, cut the butter in until it is in mostly pea-size pieces. A few large stray chunks are fine to remain. Add in the pecans and cream. Use a wooden spoon to stir it all together until the mixture has just begun to hold itself. It shouldn't be well incorporated, but rough, with a fair few dry-floured pockets remaining. Tip onto a floured work surface.

Use your hands to gather the dough together, incorporating as much of the dry bits as possible. It'll seem hard to handle at first, like it won't come together, but it will as you continue to work it. Pat into a rough moundlike shape that's about 1 inch (2.5 cm) thick, then fold in half over itself, give it a quarter turn, and reshape again. Repeat this process three more times, until the dough has made a full rotation, then shape it into a circle about the same dimensions above. Cut the circle into quarters, then each quarter in half, to form eight even triangles. Freeze until firm, about 20 minutes. Meanwhile, preheat the oven to 400°F (200°C).

When you're ready to bake, divide the scones between the prepared sheets. Use a pastry brush to coat them in a light wash of cream.

Bake for 20 to 22 minutes, rotating the sheets top to bottom and bottom to top halfway through, until golden brown. Let the scones stand on the sheet for a few minutes, before transferring them to a wire rack to cool further.

Meanwhile, make the glaze. Whisk together the confectioners' sugar, maple syrup, butter, vanilla, cinnamon, and salt until smooth. Spoon over the tops of the scones. They're best eaten soon after making but will keep covered on the counter for up to 3 days.

FOR THE SCONES

½ CUP (70 G) COARSELY CHOPPED PECANS

3 CUPS (375 G) ALL-PURPOSE FLOUR, *PLUS EXTRA FOR THE WORK SURFACE*

1 TABLESPOON BAKING POWDER

2½ TEASPOONS GROUND CINNAMON

½ TEASPOON SALT

⅓ CUP + 1 TABLESPOON (90 G) LIGHT BROWN SUGAR

½ CUP + 1 TABLESPOON (1 STICK + 1 TABLESPOON; 130 G) UNSALTED BUTTER, *COLD AND CUT INTO ½-INCH (12-MM) CUBES*

1 CUP (240 ML) HEAVY CREAM, *PLUS EXTRA FOR BRUSHING*

FOR THE GLAZE

¾ CUP (90 G) CONFECTIONERS' SUGAR

2 TABLESPOONS PURE MAPLE SYRUP

1 TABLESPOON UNSALTED BUTTER, *MELTED*

½ TEASPOON VANILLA EXTRACT

¼ TEASPOON GROUND CINNAMON

A PINCH OF SALT

sugared sesame banana bread

makes an 8 x 4-inch (21 x 11-cm) loaf, which serves eight to ten

I never want to be without tahini. It's one of those things that I could eat forever, never tiring of it. It's rich and astringent, with a creaminess that seems to make everything taste just a bit better. I've put it in this, along with some sesame oil, which takes it further than banana bread. It's heaven.

Preheat the oven to 350°F (180°C). Grease and line an 8 x 4 x 2½-inch (20 x 10 x 6-cm) loaf pan with parchment paper, leaving a slight overhang on both sides.

Put the bananas into a medium bowl and use a fork to mash them up, almost to a fine pulp. Slice the extra banana half, in half, lengthwise, then set both pieces aside for the top.

Sift together the flour, baking soda, and salt.

In a separate mixing bowl, whisk together the brown sugar, eggs, tahini, vegetable oil, sesame oil, vanilla, and sour cream until smooth. Whisk in the mashed banana. Tip in the dry ingredients, then use a large rubber spatula, along with a strong guiding hand, to fold until just incorporated, being careful not to overmix.

Scrape the batter into the prepared pan and rest the reserved banana pieces over the top. Scatter with granulated sugar.

Bake for about an hour, until golden brown and a skewer inserted into the middle comes out clean. Let cool in the pan for 15 minutes, before lifting it out and onto a wire rack to cool completely.

⅓ CUP + 1 TEASPOON (80 ML) VEGETABLE OIL, *PLUS EXTRA FOR GREASING THE PAN*

ABOUT 3 MEDIUM-RIPE BANANAS (320 G), *PLUS ANOTHER HALF SET ASIDE FOR THE TOP*

1¾ CUPS (220 G) ALL-PURPOSE FLOUR

1 TEASPOON BAKING SODA

½ TEASPOON SALT

1 CUP PACKED (220 G) LIGHT BROWN SUGAR

2 LARGE EGGS

⅓ CUP (90 G) TAHINI

1 TABLESPOON SESAME OIL

1 TEASPOON VANILLA EXTRACT

½ CUP + 1 TABLESPOON (135 G) SOUR CREAM

1½ TABLESPOONS GRANULATED SUGAR

malt and buckwheat ice cream

serves four to six

I love buckwheat. I eat it almost every day, but the best is in ice cream. This is rich and nutty, with a deep, caramelized tone from brown sugar and, surprisingly, malt. It never seems to last long and you'd be wise to make double, if you and your churner can handle it.

Put the buckwheat into a nonstick skillet. Toast, shaking often, until browned and fragrant. Transfer it into a large saucepan, along with the cream and milk. Bring to a simmer, then remove and set aside to steep for 20 minutes, giving it a gentle stir every so often to prevent a skin from forming.

Strain the mixture through a fine-mesh sieve and into a bowl, using the back of a spoon to press on the buckwheat to help release any infused juices, then discard it. Pour back into the saucepan and whisk in the malt. Let the mixture return to a simmer. Meanwhile, whisk the egg yolks and sugar in a medium-size heatproof bowl.

Slip a little stream of the hot cream into the yolks, whisking well to acclimatize them to the heat, then pour it all back into the saucepan set on the stove. Continue to cook, stirring constantly, until it is thick enough to coat the back of a spoon. It shouldn't take more than a few minutes. Remove and stir in the vanilla and salt. Again, strain the mixture into a large bowl, then cover the surface with a layer of plastic wrap to prevent a skin from forming. Chill until cold, at least 8 hours but preferably overnight.

The next morning, churn in a machine according to the manufacturer's instructions. It'll be near doubled with a supple, almost soft serve–like consistency when it's done. Scrape into a container, cover, and freeze until just firm before serving.

2/3 CUP (115 G) RAW BUCKWHEAT

2 CUPS (480 ML) HEAVY CREAM

1 2/3 CUPS (400 ML) WHOLE MILK

1/4 CUP (30 G) MALTED MILK POWDER

6 LARGE EGG YOLKS

1/2 CUP + 1 TABLESPOON PACKED (125 G) LIGHT BROWN SUGAR

1 TEASPOON VANILLA EXTRACT

1/2 TEASPOON SALT

cinnamon buns

makes eighteen buns

These are meant to rival a morning bun. They're made with brioche dough instead of croissant, and have all the best qualities of one, but without a lot of the fuss. Soft, spiced, and sticky-sweet, they're wonderful.

Grease two 12-cup muffin pans with butter, then toss in a little granulated sugar, shaking until each indent is well coated. Tap out the excess.

Set the brioche dough onto a floured work surface, dusting the top lightly too. With a rolling pin, begin to roll it into a rough rectangle shape that's about 16 x 14 inches (40 x 35 cm) in size, or 1 inch (2.5 cm) thick. Slick with melted butter then scatter the brown sugar, 1 tablespoon of the cinnamon, and the salt. Smear the topping almost to the edges.

Starting with the longest edge away from you, roll the dough into a taut log-shaped cylinder, pinching the edges together to seal. Turn it seam side down. Use a sharp knife to trim off the edges, then slice it into equal-sized pieces that are about 1 inch (2.5 cm) thick. Gently fit into the muffin cups, then cover, and leave to rise until almost doubled in size, about half an hour.

Meanwhile, set oven racks in the lower and upper thirds of the oven. Preheat to 350°F (180°C). Combine the granulated sugar and remaining teaspoon of cinnamon in a shallow bowl, for coating, and set aside. Once the buns have risen, brush them with egg wash, using a light touch so not to deflate them.

Bake for 18 to 22 minutes, rotating halfway through, until golden brown. Let the buns cool for a few minutes, then use a blunt knife to help ease them out of the pan and onto a wire rack. Toss in the cinnamon sugar, one at a time, until coated. Serve soon after, warm.

BRIOCHE DOUGH (*SEE PAGE 224*)

FLOUR FOR THE WORK SURFACE

¼ CUP (½ STICK; 60 G) UNSALTED BUTTER, *MELTED, PLUS EXTRA FOR GREASING THE PANS*

½ CUP (100 G) GRANULATED SUGAR, *PLUS EXTRA FOR THE PANS*

⅔ CUP PACKED (150 G) LIGHT BROWN SUGAR

1 TABLESPOON + 1 TEASPOON GROUND CINNAMON

A PINCH OF SALT

1 LARGE EGG, *BEATEN, FOR THE EGG WASH*

brown sugar cheesecake

makes a 9-inch (23-cm) cake, which serves eight to twelve

This will be one of the greatest cheesecakes you'll ever make. The inspiration for it comes from Fanny Zanotti's *Paris Pastry Club*, which has a similar cake that I'd always loved to make. It has a silky, supple, and almost velvet-like texture, that seems to get better with each bite. The recipe is straightforward, but it does require some forethought, as it's baked at a low heat for a long time. Now is the season for slowing; yield to it.

Set an oven rack in the middle of the oven. Preheat to 350°F (180°C). Grease and line a 9-inch (23-cm) round springform cake pan with parchment paper, covering the outside of it in a few layers of aluminum foil. Bring a kettle of water to a boil.

To make the crust, put the graham cracker crumbs, hazelnuts, and salt into a medium bowl. Stir in the melted butter until evenly moistened. Tip the mixture into the prepared pan, using the back of a spoon to press it into an even layer. Bake for 10 to 12 minutes until golden brown. Set aside to cool.

Lower the oven temperature to 250°F (120°C). Pour enough boiling water into a deep roasting dish until it's about half full, then set it on the bottom of the oven.

In the bowl of a stand mixer fitted with the paddle attachment, beat the cream cheese until smooth and malleable, about a minute. Add the sugar and beat until light caramel in color. Pause mixing to scrape down the bottom and side of the bowl. Add the eggs, one at a time, beating well to incorporate each addition, then beat in the vanilla and liqueur, if using. Add the sour cream. Beat until a silky-smooth batter has formed. Strain through a fine-mesh sieve over the cooled crust, using an offset palette knife to smooth it out.

Bake for 1 to 1¼ hours, until just set. It should still have a slight wiggle to it. Turn off the oven and remove the roasting dish of water. Allow the cheesecake to remain inside with the door ajar, until it reaches room temperature, about another hour. Transfer to the refrigerator to chill until cold, at least 6 hours but preferably overnight.

When you're ready to serve, carefully release the cake from the pan and slide it onto a plate, peeling off the paper. Adorn with crystallized nuts. It will keep, covered in the refrigerator, for about 3 days.

FOR THE CRUST

3 TABLESPOONS UNSALTED BUTTER, *MELTED, PLUS EXTRA UNMELTED FOR GREASING THE PAN*

¾ CUP + 1½ TABLESPOONS (110 G) GRAHAM CRACKER CRUMBS

⅓ CUP (30 G) GROUND HAZELNUTS

A PINCH OF SALT

FOR THE FILLING

2¼ CUPS (500 G) CREAM CHEESE

½ CUP (110 G) LIGHT BROWN SUGAR

3 LARGE EGGS

1 TEASPOON VANILLA EXTRACT

2 TABLESPOONS HAZELNUT LIQUEUR, *OPTIONAL*

¾ CUP (180 ML) SOUR CREAM

CRYSTALLIZED NUTS, *FOR DECORATING (SEE PAGE 226)*

buckwheat
chocolate chunk cookies

makes about thirty-two cookies

These are my ideal. They're crisp, golden, and molten with chocolate. Made with buckwheat too, for its warm, nutty undertone. Because of how much I love them, I often start the dough ahead of time, then bake it from frozen, on whim. That's warm cookies in an instant, a true pleasure.

Whisk together the all-purpose and buckwheat flours, baking powder, baking soda, and salt.

Put the butter in a medium-size saucepan set over medium-low heat. Heat, stirring often, until melted. Pour into a large bowl, then add the sugars. Whisk until combined. Whisk in the egg, followed by the vanilla, until smooth and glossy. Tip in the dry ingredients and, with a wooden spoon, beat until a soft dough has begun to form. Mix in the chocolate. Transfer to the refrigerator to chill until firm, at least 30 minutes.

Meanwhile, set oven racks in the lower and upper thirds of the oven. Preheat to 350°F (180°C). Line two baking sheets with parchment paper.

Use a scoop or tablespoon to portion out evenly sized amounts of the dough. If you're using a spoon, use your hands to roll them into balls. Divide between the prepared sheets, placing them a few inches apart to allow for spreading. You should be able to fit 8 to 10 per sheet. Sprinkle a pinch of sea salt over the tops. You can set leftover dough aside to be baked off later, or store in an airtight container and freeze for up to two months. Allow to stand at room temperature for about 15 minutes before baking from frozen.

Bake for 10 to 12 minutes, rotating the sheets from top to bottom and bottom to top halfway through, until golden, the edges crisp but the centers soft. Let the cookies stand on the sheet for a few minutes, before transferring them off and onto a wire rack to cool further before serving.

2 CUPS (250 G) ALL-PURPOSE FLOUR

⅔ CUP (80 G) BUCKWHEAT FLOUR

1¼ TEASPOONS BAKING POWDER

1 TEASPOON BAKING SODA

1 TEASPOON SALT

¾ CUP + 2 TABLESPOONS (1½ STICKS + 2 TABLESPOONS; 200 G) UNSALTED BUTTER

1 CUP (220 G) LIGHT BROWN SUGAR

⅔ CUP (135 G) GRANULATED SUGAR

1 LARGE EGG

1 TABLESPOON VANILLA EXTRACT

1¼ CUPS (215 G) COARSELY CHOPPED DARK CHOCOLATE

SEA SALT FLAKES, *FOR FINISHING*

rye bark

serves six

This idea comes from my good friend Claire Ptak. I remember the first time we met, and it was like we'd known each other all along. Words can't express how much she means to me. Chocolate and bread may seem an odd match, but I promise it's anything but. Both are warm, grounding, and familiar, a feet-on-the-earth kind of thing. Use the best you can find, like a good, dark rye and chocolate to match.

Preheat the oven to 350°F (180°C). Line a baking sheet with parchment paper.

Toss the rye bread into a food processor and blitz to form fine crumbs. It's fine if a few larger pieces remain. Scatter onto the prepared sheet. Toast, stirring halfway through, until golden brown, about 10 minutes. Remove and let cool completely.

Put 1⅔ cups (285 g) of the chocolate into a large heatproof bowl set over a saucepan filled with a few inches of barely simmering water. Do not allow the base of the bowl to touch the water below. Heat, stirring often, until almost all of it has melted. Remove the bowl and tip in the remaining chocolate, giving it a good, vigorous stir, until melted. Stir through the bread crumbs.

Tip onto the baking sheet, using an offset palette knife to smooth it into an even layer. Sprinkle over the salt.

Chill until set, about 10 to 15 minutes, depending on thickness. Use your fingers to break the chocolate slab up into splintered, bark-like shards before serving. It can be kept at room temperature in a cool and dark place, but if it's too humid, keep cold in the refrigerator. It will keep for about 1 week.

1¾ CUPS (60 G) TORN RYE BREAD

2½ CUPS (425 G) FINELY CHOPPED COUVERTURE MILK CHOCOLATE

SEA SALT FLAKES, *FOR FINISHING*

brutti ma buoni

makes about fifteen cookies

Crackled, chewy, and crisp, these meringue cookies are far more than their "ugly but good" name suggests and are ideal for using up leftover egg whites from the yolk-enriched recipes in this book.

Set oven racks in the lower and upper thirds of the oven. Preheat the oven to 350°F (180°C). Line two large baking sheets with parchment paper.

Scatter the hazelnuts onto one of the sheets and roast until brown, 10 to 12 minutes. Set aside to cool. Lower the oven temperature to 325°F (160°C). Transfer the nuts to a food processor along with ½ cup + 2 tablespoons (125 g) of the sugar. Pulse to a coarse meal. Tip into a large bowl.

Put the egg whites and salt into the bowl of a stand mixer fitted with the whisk attachment. Whisk, on medium-high speed, until foamy, then scatter in the remaining sugar, a tablespoon at a time, until a stiff and glossy meringue has formed. Fold into the hazelnuts until just combined. Scrape the mixture into a large saucepan.

Transfer the saucepan to the stove and heat, over low, until the mixture has become thick enough to pull away from the side of the pan, about 10 minutes. Be sure to stir constantly to prevent the mixture from catching then burning. It should be dried out and a few shades darker in color than when it started.

Use a generous tablespoon to scoop out evenly sized portions of the mixture onto the prepared sheets, placing them a few inches apart, and piling them into mounds, as neat and tight as you can get them. It will firm as it cools, so you'll want to move quickly. If you find the mixture is getting difficult to work with, clean the spoon off every so often.

Bake for 25 to 30 minutes, rotating the pans top to bottom and bottom to top halfway through, until the cookies are light fawn in color and crackled. Transfer to a wire rack and let cool on the sheets until crisp before serving.

1¾ CUPS (250 G) COARSELY CHOPPED HAZELNUTS

1¼ CUPS (250 G) GRANULATED SUGAR

4 LARGE EGG WHITES

A PINCH OF SALT

double crumb halvah cake

Makes an 8 x 4-inch (21 x 11-cm) loaf, which serves eight to ten

It's cakes like this that I love most. They're rustic, filled with comfort, heart, and not fussy at all. Halvah is a dense sweet made from sesame and it makes this cake especially good. It starts to dissolve during baking, turning into this molten mess that stickily seeps into the crumb. It's addictive, and if I'm honest, I'm in it for that alone.

Preheat the oven to 350°F (180°C). Grease and line an 8 x 4 x 3-inch (21 x 11 x 7-cm) loaf pan with parchment paper, leaving a slight overhang on both sides.

First, make the crumb. Put the flour, sugar, cinnamon, and salt in a medium bowl. Add in the butter and use your fingers to rub it in until rough, damp clumps have formed. Stir through the walnuts, then set aside.

To make the cake, whisk together the flour, cinnamon, baking soda, baking powder, and salt.

In the bowl of a stand mixer fitted with the paddle attachment, beat the butter and sugar on medium speed until pale caramel in color, about 3 minutes. Pause mixing to scrape down the bottom and side of the bowl. Add in the eggs, one at a time, beating well to incorporate each addition, then beat in the sesame oil and vanilla. Set the speed to low. Beat in half of the dry ingredients, followed by all the sour cream, then beat in the remaining dry ingredients until well combined.

Scrape half of the batter into the prepared pan, using an offset palette knife to smooth it out. Scatter over half the crumb, then use your fingers to break the halvah up into chunks, scattering it over too. Cover with the remaining batter and crumb.

Bake for 45 to 50 minutes, until golden brown. A skewer inserted into the middle should come out almost clean with a few moist crumbs attached to it. Let the cake cool in the pan for 15 minutes before lifting it out and onto a wire rack to cool further. Finish with a good dusting of confectioners' sugar before serving.

FOR THE CRUMB

½ CUP + 1 TABLESPOON (70 G) ALL-PURPOSE FLOUR

¼ CUP PACKED (55 G) LIGHT BROWN SUGAR

¼ TEASPOON GROUND CINNAMON

A PINCH OF SALT

¼ CUP (½ STICK; 60 G) UNSALTED BUTTER, *MELTED*

⅓ CUP (45 G) CHOPPED ROASTED WALNUTS

FOR THE CAKE

½ CUP (1 STICK; 115 G) UNSALTED BUTTER, *SOFTENED AT ROOM TEMPERATURE, PLUS EXTRA FOR GREASING THE PAN*

1¼ CUPS + 1 TEASPOON (160 G) ALL-PURPOSE FLOUR

1 TEASPOON GROUND CINNAMON

¾ TEASPOON BAKING SODA

½ TEASPOON BAKING POWDER

½ TEASPOON SALT

¾ CUP PACKED (165 G) LIGHT BROWN SUGAR

2 LARGE EGGS

1 TABLESPOON SESAME OIL

1 TEASPOON VANILLA EXTRACT

¾ CUP (180 G) SOUR CREAM

½ CUP (80 G) HALVAH

CONFECTIONERS' SUGAR, *FOR FINISHING*

bay leaf blondies

makes nine to twelve blondies

If I could distill the woodland, it would be in these. They're grounded.
It's the bay that does it. The leaves have an aromatic taste of the earth,
that balances out the often sickly sweet white chocolate perfectly. Be sure
to finish them with salt. It brings it all together.

Preheat the oven to 350°F (180°C). Grease and line an 8-inch (20-cm) square
baking pan with parchment paper, allowing an overhang on the sides.

Put the butter and bay leaves into a deep saucepan. Heat on medium,
stirring often, until the butter is melted. Turn the heat to medium-high
and continue to cook, swirling the pan often but not stirring, until a
deep-amber-hued liquid has formed. It will foam, hiss, and crackle but
should subside as it nears done. Pour into a bowl, straining out the leaves
and scraping in any burnt bits that have formed at the base of the pan.
Whisk in the sugar, then whisk in the eggs, one at a time, until glossy.
Whisk in the vanilla and salt.

With a fine-mesh sieve, sift in the flour, then use a large rubber spatula
to fold until just combined. Fold in the chocolate. Scrape into the prepared
pan, using an offset palette knife to smooth it into an even layer. Press a few
leaves on top then sprinkle with salt.

Bake for 30 minutes, until golden, crackled, and shiny. The edges should
be firm and the middle just set, but still slightly gooey. Let cool in the pan
completely, before lifting out and slicing into squares. Remove the leaves
before eating. The blondies will keep well, covered on the counter, for up to
3 days.

¾ CUP + 2 TABLESPOONS
(1½ STICKS + 2 TABLESPOONS;
200 G) UNSALTED BUTTER, *PLUS
EXTRA FOR GREASING THE PAN*

3 DRIED BAY LEAVES, *PLUS A
FEW FOR THE TOP*

1½ CUPS (330 G) LIGHT BROWN
SUGAR

2 LARGE EGGS

1 TABLESPOON VANILLA EXTRACT

½ TEASPOON SALT

1½ CUPS (190 G) ALL-PURPOSE
FLOUR

1 CUP + 3 TABLESPOONS (200 G)
COARSELY CHOPPED WHITE
CHOCOLATE

SEA SALT FLAKES, *FOR FINISHING*

parsnip cake
with tahini frosting

makes an 8-inch (20-cm) cake, which serves eight to twelve

When parsnips are baked, they become sweet and wood-ish, caramelized too. They're ideal for cake like this, which tastes of the earth in the best possible way. It's all about the frosting, though, and you'd be hard-pressed to not want to spread it over everything. The recipe will make enough to frost thick or thin, but in this case, the more, the better, I think.

Preheat the oven to 350°F (180°C). Grease and line two 8-inch (20-cm) round cake pans with parchment paper.

To make the cake, sift together the flour, baking powder, baking soda, cinnamon, cardamom, nutmeg, allspice, ginger, cloves, salt, and orange zest.

In the bowl of a stand mixer fitted with the whisk attachment, whisk the eggs and sugar on medium speed until light caramel in color, about 3 minutes. It should be thick enough to hold a trail too. Set the speed to low and stream in the oil, slowly, until it is all used up. Add in the dry ingredients, whisking until combined, then remove the bowl and fold in the parsnips and pecans. Scrape into the prepared pans.

Bake for 25 to 30 minutes, until golden brown. A skewer inserted into the middle should come out clean. Let the cakes cool in the pans for about 15 minutes before turning them out and onto a wire rack to cool completely. Use a sharp serrated knife to level off any domed tops, if needed.

For the frosting, beat the butter and cream cheese together until smooth and malleable. Add in the tahini, vanilla, salt, and confectioners' sugar. Beat for a few more minutes, until a fluffy frosting has formed.

When you're ready to serve, put the first cake layer, top facing up, onto a serving plate. Spread a generous amount of frosting then top with the second layer, cut side facing down. Cover the cake in a thick blanket of frosting, then chill until set before serving, about 20 minutes.

FOR THE CAKE

1 CUP + 1 TABLESPOON (240 ML) VEGETABLE OIL, *PLUS EXTRA FOR GREASING THE PAN*

1¾ CUPS + 1½ TABLESPOONS (230 G) ALL-PURPOSE FLOUR

1¼ TEASPOONS BAKING POWDER

1 TEASPOON BAKING SODA

2 TEASPOONS GROUND CINNAMON

½ TEASPOON GROUND CARDAMOM

½ TEASPOON GROUND NUTMEG

¼ TEASPOON GROUND ALLSPICE

¼ TEASPOON GROUND GINGER

A PINCH OF GROUND CLOVES

½ TEASPOON SALT

ZEST OF AN ORANGE

3 LARGE EGGS

1¼ CUPS PACKED (275 G) LIGHT BROWN SUGAR

2½ CUPS + 2 TABLESPOONS (260 G) GRATED PARSNIPS

⅔ CUP (80 G) CHOPPED ROASTED PECANS

FOR THE FROSTING

¾ CUP (1½ STICKS; 170 G) UNSALTED BUTTER, *SOFTENED AT ROOM TEMPERATURE*

⅔ CUP (150 G) CREAM CHEESE, *AT ROOM TEMPERATURE*

¾ CUP (180 G) TAHINI

1 TEASPOON VANILLA EXTRACT

A PINCH OF SALT

3 CUPS (360 G) CONFECTIONERS' SUGAR

fallen chocolate cake

makes an 8-inch (20-cm) cake, which serves eight to twelve

There's a strength in breaking apart, and nothing could be truer for this cake. It fractures as it cools, the weight proving too much to bear. The result is a ganache-like interior that's dense, dark, and smudged with coffee. Its appearance is far from perfect, but that's what makes it special. It's resilient.

Preheat the oven to 350°F (180°C). Grease and line an 8-inch (20-cm) round springform cake pan with parchment paper.

Put the butter and chocolate in a large heatproof bowl set over a saucepan filled with a few inches of barely simmering water. Do not let the base of the bowl touch the water below. Heat, stirring often, until melted. Remove and mix in the coffee and salt.

In the bowl of a stand mixer fitted with the whisk attachment, whisk the egg yolks and ⅓ cup (70 g) of the sugar on medium speed until pale, thick, and almost doubled in volume, about 3 minutes. It should be able to hold a trail when the whisk is lifted, before falling back onto itself softly. Fold into the chocolate mixture.

Clean and dry the whisk and bowl, then add the egg whites and whisk until foamy. Scatter in the remaining sugar, a tablespoon at a time, until it is all used up. Continue to whisk until a soft but stable meringue has formed. With a light touch, fold a third of it into the chocolate mixture to loosen, then fold in another third, followed by the last third, until just incorporated. Scrape into the prepared pan.

Bake for about 30 minutes, until the edges are set and the top crackled. It won't be done through completely and should still have a fair wobble to it. Transfer to a wire rack to cool. It will collapse as it does; let it.

When you're ready to serve the cake, unmold, slide it onto a plate, and peel off the paper. It'll be fragile, so handle with care. Dust the top with cocoa powder. Keep covered, cold or on the counter, for up to 3 days.

⅔ CUP (1¼ STICKS + 1 TEASPOON; 150 G) UNSALTED BUTTER, *PLUS EXTRA FOR GREASING THE PAN*

2 CUPS (340 G) FINELY CHOPPED DARK CHOCOLATE

2 TABLESPOONS HOT COFFEE

¼ TEASPOON SALT

5 LARGE EGGS, *SEPARATED*

⅔ CUP (135 G) GRANULATED SUGAR

DUTCH PROCESSED COCOA POWDER, *FOR FINISHING*

SMOKE

"Once in the fire one is bathed in sweetness."
—HÉLÈNE CIXOUS, *The Book of Promethea*

WINTER IS KNOWN to assault the senses, but if there's anything it teaches us, it's that not all lies dormant. It turns us ravenous. Thirsts become deeper; hungers, greater; and desires, stronger. Smoke is synonymous with the new season, for fire is at its heart. It's primal. Who we are, what we are, stripped down to the core. I've always thought that the body eats but the spirit remembers, and smoke sates some savage within, however deep or buried.

It's comforting and familiar, but with a bad reputation. I don't think it's as overpowering or narcotic as it's made out to be; instead subtle, secretive, and shy. It likes to sit in the back of things, brooding, and to define the true nature of it is nothing but difficult. Not just soot, ash, or smog, but elemental and earthen, with a rather feverish undertone; it's complex.

And therein lies its beauty. It's elusive and hard to tame. We can't hold it as we can other aromatics, like spices, zests, or florals, but make no mistake: it is an aromatic, and one that should be used. In fact, we've been relying on it to enhance food for almost ever. It doesn't just need to come from fire, as it can be found in a lot of other ingredients too, like coffee, nuts, chocolate, and salt, as well as tea, sugar, alcohol, and grains.

It has to be harnessed, though, soothed, treated, and rustled, to come alive, and ultimately, that's not something that can be taught, but must be felt.

smoked fleur de sel brownies

makes nine to twelve brownies

Unadulterated describes these best. They're intense and strong, but refined, because of a pinch of smoked fleur de sel, which stands up well to sweetness. I think brownies are always best made pure, with nothing but chocolate, but if you were to throw a handful of walnuts into the mix, I don't think there'd be any complaints.

Preheat the oven to 350°F (180°C). Grease and line an 8-inch (20-cm) square baking pan with parchment paper, leaving a slight overhang on the sides.

Put the chocolate into a large bowl, setting it aside but near the space where you'll be working. Melt the butter in a saucepan over medium heat. Heat, stirring often, until melted. Raise the heat to medium-high and continue to cook, swirling the pan often but not stirring, until a deep-amber-hued liquid has formed. It will foam, hiss, and crackle at first, but subside as it nears done. Pour into the bowl with the chocolate, scraping in any burnt bits that have formed at the base of the saucepan, then stir until smooth.

In the bowl of a stand mixer fitted with the whisk attachment, whisk the sugar, eggs, and vanilla on medium-high speed until pale, thick, and doubled in volume, 3 to 4 minutes. Meanwhile, sift together the cocoa, flour, espresso, and salt. Lower the speed and stream in the melted chocolate, slowly, until it is all used up. Tip in the dry ingredients and whisk until almost incorporated. Some streaks should remain. Remove the bowl from the stand mixer and with a large rubber spatula, finish mixing the batter together by hand until it is smooth, thick, and glossy. Smooth into the prepared pan and sprinkle with fleur de sel.

Bake for about 25 minutes, until the edges are set. The middle should still have a slight squidge to it and the top should be shiny too. Let the brownie cool in the pan completely before lifting it out and cutting into squares. They will keep well, stored in an airtight container at room temperature, for up to 3 days.

¾ CUP + 2 TABLESPOONS (1½ STICKS + 2 TABLESPOONS; 200 G) UNSALTED BUTTER, *PLUS EXTRA FOR GREASING THE PAN*

⅔ CUP (115 G) FINELY CHOPPED DARK CHOCOLATE

1½ CUPS (300 G) GRANULATED SUGAR

3 LARGE EGGS, *COLD*

1 TABLESPOON VANILLA EXTRACT

¾ CUP + 1 TABLESPOON (80 G) DUTCH PROCESSED COCOA POWDER

½ CUP + 1 TEASPOON (70 G) ALL-PURPOSE FLOUR

1 TEASPOON ESPRESSO POWDER

½ TEASPOON SALT

SMOKED FLEUR DE SEL, *FOR FINISHING*

tiramisu

serves ten to twelve

Tiramisu should be boozy and rich, with a deep creaminess to it, which is entirely how I like it. It's a simple thing, and as such, there's nowhere to hide. The ingredients are important. Pick a smooth, almost clotted cream–like mascarpone and a good, strong espresso. I prefer to use glasses for serving it, but you could do it up in a large dish too. It's forgiving.

First, make the cream. Put the mascarpone, cream, rum, egg yolks, vanilla, and sugar in the bowl of a stand mixer fitted with the whisk attachment. Whisk, on medium speed, until soft peaks have formed. You want it to retain a slight flow, so that if you drag your finger through it, it leaves a supple, almost ribbonlike trail.

In a separate bowl, whisk the egg whites until soft but stable peaks have formed, being careful not to overwhisk them. With a gentle hand and a rubber spatula, fold a third into the mascarpone mixture, until almost combined, then fold in another third, followed by the last, until incorporated.

To assemble, set out as many dishes as you'll need, or use a large one. Coat the bases in a thin layer of the mascarpone cream. Swirl a savoiardi biscuit in the espresso until soaked, then arrange it into the bottom of the dish. Repeat with enough biscuits to cover, then spread over a good amount of mascarpone cream, to coat. Form more layers in the same manner as above, until everything is used up. Tiramisu is at its best when it's had time to meld, so chill for at least 6 hours, but preferably overnight.

Serve dusted in a thick layer of cocoa.

FOR THE CREAM

2¼ CUPS (500 G) MASCARPONE

⅓ CUP (80 ML) HEAVY CREAM

2 TABLESPOONS RUM

5 LARGE EGGS, *SEPARATED*

1 TEASPOON VANILLA EXTRACT

½ CUP + 2 TABLESPOONS (125 G) GRANULATED SUGAR

ABOUT 24 SAVOIARDI BISCUITS OR LADYFINGERS

1½ CUPS (360 ML) STRONG BREWED ESPRESSO

DUTCH PROCESSED COCOA POWDER, *FOR FINISHING*

walnut snowballs

makes about twenty

Heat seems to transform the flavor profile of a walnut completely, turning it into something more bitter, tannic, and smoked. They're lovely in these snowballs, which are sweet enough to balance out the strength.

Set oven racks in the lower and upper thirds of the oven. Preheat to 350°F (180°C). Line two large baking sheets with parchment paper.

Scatter the walnuts onto one of the sheets. Roast until brown, 10 to 12 minutes, then set aside to cool. Transfer into the bowl of a food processor and process to a fine meal, being careful not to overprocess to the point of damp clumps. It shouldn't take more than 15 seconds. Combine with the flour and salt in a medium-size bowl.

In the bowl of a stand mixer fitted with the paddle attachment, beat the butter and vanilla seeds on medium speed until smooth, then tip in ½ cup + 2 tablespoons (75 g) of the confectioners' sugar. Beat, until pale and creamy, about 3 minutes. Pause mixing to scrape down the bottom and side of the bowl. Set the speed to low. Tip in the dry ingredients and beat until a soft dough has just begun to form. Cover and transfer to the refrigerator to chill for at least 30 minutes.

Meanwhile, preheat the oven to 325°F (160°C). Put the remaining confectioners' sugar in a shallow bowl for coating.

With a teaspoon as a measure, scoop out generous portions of the dough, then use your hands to roll each into balls. If you have a scale, they should each be about 20 grams in weight. Divide between the prepared sheets, placing them a few inches apart, as they'll puff up during baking.

Bake for 15 to 17 minutes, rotating top to bottom and bottom to top halfway through, until light golden brown. Allow to cool on the sheets for a few minutes, before rolling each in the sugar, one at a time, until coated. Transfer to a wire rack and let the coating set. Roll again, for a final time. They'll keep well, stored in an airtight container at room temperature, for about a week.

⅔ CUP + 3 TABLESPOONS (100 G) WALNUTS

1½ CUPS + 1½ TABLESPOONS (200 G) ALL-PURPOSE FLOUR

¼ TEASPOON SALT

⅔ CUP (1¼ STICKS + 1 TEASPOON; 150 G) UNSALTED BUTTER, *SOFTENED AT ROOM TEMPERATURE*

SEEDS OF A VANILLA BEAN POD

1⅓ CUPS (160 G) CONFECTIONERS' SUGAR

burnt sugar ice cream

serves four to six

I have a palate that borders on burnt. I learnt it from my mother, and she, from her mother. It's a vice and, dare I think, a Russian one. We don't do light. I remember my grandmother burning sugar for me when I was sick, as a child. The best cure, she'd say. I never forgot the taste of it, and it reminds me of this ice cream. Push the burn as far as you can, for best results.

Pour the cream, milk, and orange zest into a deep saucepan. Give it a stir to combine, then let it come to a simmer over low heat. Meanwhile, put 1 cup (200 g) of the sugar into a separate saucepan, along with the water. Cook over medium heat, swirling the pan often but not stirring, until dark amber in color. You'll know it's done when it looks and smells like a deep, burnt caramel. While you're waiting for the sugar to scorch, whisk the yolks and remaining sugar together in a medium-size heatproof bowl.

Pour the burnt sugar into the cream, whisking constantly to combine. It'll seize as it's added but will come together as it heats. Slip a stream of the mixture into the yolks, whisking to acclimatize them to the heat, then pour all of it back into the saucepan. Continue to cook, stirring constantly, until thick enough to coat the back of a spoon. It shouldn't take more than a few minutes. Remove and stir in the Grand Marnier, if using, and salt. Pour into a large bowl, covering the surface with plastic wrap to prevent a skin from forming. Chill until cold, at least 8 hours but preferably overnight.

Churn in an ice cream machine according to the manufacturer's instructions. It should be thick, creamy, and voluminous when it's done. Scrape into a container, cover, and freeze until firm before serving.

2 CUPS (480 ML) HEAVY CREAM

1¾ CUPS + 2 TABLESPOONS (450 ML) WHOLE MILK

ZEST OF AN ORANGE

1¼ CUPS (250 G) GRANULATED SUGAR

¼ CUP (60 ML) WATER

6 LARGE EGG YOLKS

2 TABLESPOONS GRAND MARNIER, *OPTIONAL*

A PINCH OF SALT

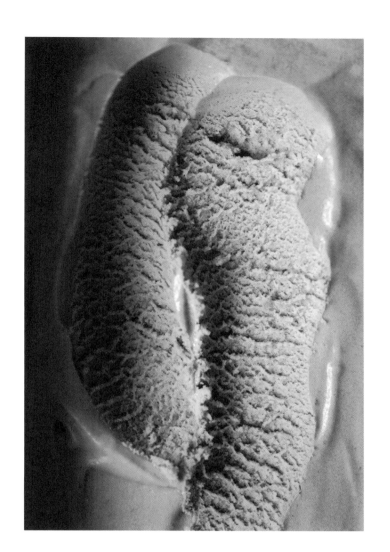

espresso marble cake

makes an 8 x 4-inch (21 x 11-cm) loaf, which serves eight to ten

This is where light and dark come to meet. It's a cake that's intense with chocolate, vanilla, and espresso, swirled together to form something wonderful. There's an urgency to how it should be eaten. Best, I think, warm and torn apart, as it has a crumb that will firm with time. It's good in all stages, though.

Preheat the oven to 350°F (180°C). Grease and line an 8 x 4 x 3-inch (21 x 11 x 7-cm) loaf pan with parchment paper, leaving a slight overhang on both sides.

To make the streusel, put the flour, sugar, cocoa, espresso, and salt in a small bowl. Add in the butter and use your fingers to rub it in until pea-size crumbs have formed. It'll seem a little dry at first but will come together as you continue to work it. Stir in the nibs, then set aside.

Next, make the cake. In a small measuring cup, stir together the espresso powder and water until dissolved. Sift the flour, baking powder, baking soda, and salt into a large mixing bowl.

In the bowl of a stand mixer fitted with the paddle attachment, beat the butter and sugar on medium speed until light and fluffy, 3 to 5 minutes. Pause to scrape down the bottom and side of the bowl. Beat in the eggs, one at a time, then beat in the vanilla. Set the speed to low. Beat in half of the dry ingredients, followed by all the sour cream, then the remainder of the dry ingredients. Set the speed back to medium and beat until aerated.

Transfer a quarter of the batter into a small bowl and add in the dissolved espresso and the cocoa. Work the mixture together with a wooden spoon until smooth.

Using a generous tablespoon, begin to drop alternating dollops of the batters into the prepared pan, in a checkerboard-like manner, until they're all used up. Use a skewer to swirl them into each other to create a marbled effect, being careful not to overdo it, as too much of a drag could muddy it. Cover with the streusel.

Bake for 50 to 55 minutes, until golden brown. A skewer inserted into the middle should come out clean. Let the cake cool in the pan for 15 minutes before lifting it out and onto a wire rack to cool further. Dust with confectioners' sugar before serving.

FOR THE STREUSEL

¼ CUP (30 G) ALL-PURPOSE FLOUR

¼ CUP (50 G) GRANULATED SUGAR

3 TABLESPOONS (15 G) DUTCH PROCESSED COCOA POWDER

1 TEASPOON ESPRESSO POWDER

A PINCH OF SALT

2½ TABLESPOONS UNSALTED BUTTER, *COLD*

1 TABLESPOON CACAO NIBS

FOR THE CAKE

¾ CUP (1½ STICKS; 170 G) UNSALTED BUTTER, *SOFTENED AT ROOM TEMPERATURE, PLUS EXTRA FOR GREASING THE PAN*

2 TEASPOONS ESPRESSO POWDER

1 TABLESPOON HOT WATER

2 CUPS + 2 TABLESPOONS (265 G) ALL-PURPOSE FLOUR

1¼ TEASPOONS BAKING POWDER

½ TEASPOON BAKING SODA

½ TEASPOON SALT

1½ CUPS (300 G) GRANULATED SUGAR

3 LARGE EGGS

1 TABLESPOON VANILLA EXTRACT

¾ CUP + 2 TABLESPOONS (210 G) SOUR CREAM

2 TABLESPOONS DUTCH PROCESSED COCOA POWDER

CONFECTIONERS' SUGAR, *FOR FINISHING*

s'mores pie

makes a 9-inch (23-cm) pie, which serves eight to twelve

This is s'mores at its finest, but better, with ras el hanout, a fiery blend of spices. The flavor is distinct and hot, with an almost aphrodisiac quality that reminds me of long, fevered nights around the fire. I like to use a fair pinch of it for this, but it is strong, so use it with caution—at least at first.

Preheat the oven to 350°F (180°C). Set a 9-inch (23-cm) pie dish onto a baking sheet.

To make the crust, stir together the graham cracker crumbs, sugar, and salt.

Put the butter into a deep saucepan. Heat, stirring often, until melted. Turn the heat to medium-high and continue to cook, swirling the pan often but not stirring, until a deep-amber-hued liquid has formed. It will foam, hiss, and crackle but should subside as it nears done. Pour in the crumbs, stirring until everything is moistened, then tip into the pie dish. Use the back of a spoon to press it into the base and up the side.

Bake for 10 to 12 minutes, until golden brown. Set aside to cool. Lower the oven temperature to 325°F (160°C).

Next, make the filling. Place the chocolate in a large bowl and set it aside but near the space where you'll be working. Pour the cream and milk into a deep saucepan. Bring to a simmer over medium heat, then remove, and stream it into the bowl with the chocolate. Let stand for a minute to acclimatize, then whisk until smooth. Add the eggs, one at a time, whisking well to incorporate each addition, then mix in the vanilla. Strain through a fine-mesh sieve into the crust.

Bake for 25 to 30 minutes, rotating halfway through, until just set. It should be puffed and have a slight wiggle too. Let cool to room temperature before adorning with meringue.

To make the meringue, put the egg whites and sugar into the bowl of a stand mixer fitted with the whisk attachment. Set it over a saucepan filled with a few inches of barely simmering water. Do not let the base of the bowl touch the water below. Heat, whisking often, until it reaches 160°F (71°C) on a candy thermometer. The sugar should be dissolved and the mixture hot to the touch. Set the bowl on the stand mixer. Whisk on high speed until thick and glossy, about 5 minutes, then whisk in the rose ras el hanout.

Swoop the meringue over the top of the pie, using the back of a spoon to swirl it out, then singe it with a blow torch, carefully. You could use a broiler here instead. Just make sure to remove the pie as soon as the meringue has browned to prevent the filling from overcooking. It's best eaten on the day of making but can be kept in the refrigerator for up to 3 days.

FOR THE CRUST

1 CUP (130 G) GRAHAM CRACKER CRUMBS

2 TABLESPOONS GRANULATED SUGAR

¼ TEASPOON SALT

¼ CUP + 2 TEASPOONS (½ STICK + 2 TEASPOONS; 70 G) UNSALTED BUTTER

FOR THE FILLING

1½ CUPS (255 G) FINELY CHOPPED DARK CHOCOLATE

1 CUP + 2½ TABLESPOONS (280 ML) HEAVY CREAM

⅓ CUP (80 ML) WHOLE MILK

2 LARGE EGGS

1 TEASPOON VANILLA EXTRACT

FOR THE MERINGUE

2 LARGE EGG WHITES

¾ CUP (150 G) GRANULATED SUGAR

ROSE RAS EL HANOUT (*SEE PAGE 229*)

rye chocolate sablés

makes about twenty sablés

I don't think of rye as an ingredient, but instead a flavor to be harnessed. It's intriguing, with a smokiness that intensifies all that it touches. It works well in these sablés, as it likes chocolate a lot. They're dark, and pleasurable. I like that.

Whisk together the all-purpose and rye flours, cocoa, espresso powder, baking soda, and salt.

In the bowl of a stand mixer fitted with the paddle attachment, cream the butter and sugar on medium speed until pale caramel in color, about 3 minutes. Pause mixing to scrape down the bottom and side of the bowl. Set the speed to low and tip in the dry ingredients. Beat until a soft dough has just begun to form, a few seconds, then mix in the chocolate until distributed.

Scrape the dough onto a sheet of plastic wrap, then divide it in half. Shape each half into a taut log that's about 1½ inches (4 cm) wide. Chill until it is firm enough to slice, about an hour.

When you're ready to bake, set the oven racks in the lower and upper thirds of the oven. Preheat to 325°F (160°C). Line two large baking sheets with parchment paper.

Unwrap the logs and transfer them to a cutting board. Use a sharp knife to slice off ½-inch- (12-mm) thick rounds, rolling the log a little as you go to ensure that it's kept as neat and circular as possible. If you hit a chocolate chunk as you slice, the dough may fracture a bit. Just pinch it back together as needed. Divide between the prepared sheets, placing them a few inches apart to allow for spreading. Sprinkle with fleur de sel.

Bake for 10 to 12 minutes, rotating the pans top to bottom and bottom to top halfway through, until just firm around the edges. Let stand on the sheet for a few minutes before transferring off and onto a wire rack to cool completely before serving. They're best eaten soon after making but can be stored in an airtight container at room temperature for up to 5 days.

1 CUP + 1 TEASPOON (130 G) ALL-PURPOSE FLOUR

¾ CUP + 1 TEASPOON (80 G) RYE FLOUR

½ CUP (50 G) DUTCH PROCESSED COCOA POWDER

1 TEASPOON ESPRESSO POWDER

½ TEASPOON BAKING SODA

½ TEASPOON SALT

1 CUP (2 STICKS; 230 G) UNSALTED BUTTER, *SOFTENED AT ROOM TEMPERATURE*

1 CUP + 1 TABLESPOON (235 G) LIGHT BROWN SUGAR

⅔ CUP (115 G) FINELY CHOPPED DARK CHOCOLATE

FLEUR DE SEL, *FOR FINISHING*

black tahini brittle ice cream

serves four to six

This is pure smoke. Made from sesame seeds that have been roasted then ground into a paste, it has a sweet taste of soot. I like to eat it with shards of brittle, which make it even smokier, but you could do without it.

First, make the ice cream. Pour the cream and milk into a deep saucepan. Heat over medium-low, until it reaches a simmer. Meanwhile, whisk together the yolks, sugar, and tahini in a medium-size heatproof bowl.

Slip a little stream of the hot cream into the yolks, whisking well to acclimatize them to the heat, then pour it all back into the saucepan set on the stove. Continue to cook, stirring constantly, until it is thick enough to coat the back of a spoon. Do not allow it to come to a boil. It shouldn't take more than a few minutes. Remove and strain through a fine-mesh sieve into a large bowl. Cover with plastic wrap, pressing it onto the surface of the custard to prevent a skin from forming. Chill until cold, at least 8 hours but preferably overnight.

The next morning, remove the mixture from the refrigerator and give it a good stir to loosen. It will have thickened up quite a bit. Transfer to an ice cream machine and churn according to the manufacturer's instructions. It'll be thick, creamy, and doubled in volume when it's done. Scrape into a container, cover, and freeze until just firm before serving.

Next, make the brittle. Line a baking sheet with parchment paper. Lightly grease the surface of it with vegetable oil, then set it aside but near to the space where you'll be working.

Put the sugar and water in a medium saucepan. Cook, on medium heat, until it has reached a boil and begun to take on a honeyed hue around the edges of the pan. Tip in the sesame seeds. Continue to cook, until deep amber in color, about 3 more minutes. Immediately tip out and onto the prepared sheet. Leave to harden before snapping into shards and serving with the ice cream.

FOR THE ICE CREAM

1 ½ CUPS (360 ML) HEAVY CREAM

1 ½ CUPS (360 ML) WHOLE MILK

4 EGG YOLKS

½ CUP + 2 TABLESPOONS (125 G) GRANULATED SUGAR

½ CUP + 1 TABLESPOON (140 G) BLACK TAHINI

FOR THE BRITTLE

VEGETABLE OIL, *FOR GREASING*

¾ CUP (150 G) GRANULATED SUGAR

¼ CUP (60 ML) WATER

⅓ CUP + 1 TEASPOON (50 G) BLACK SESAME SEEDS

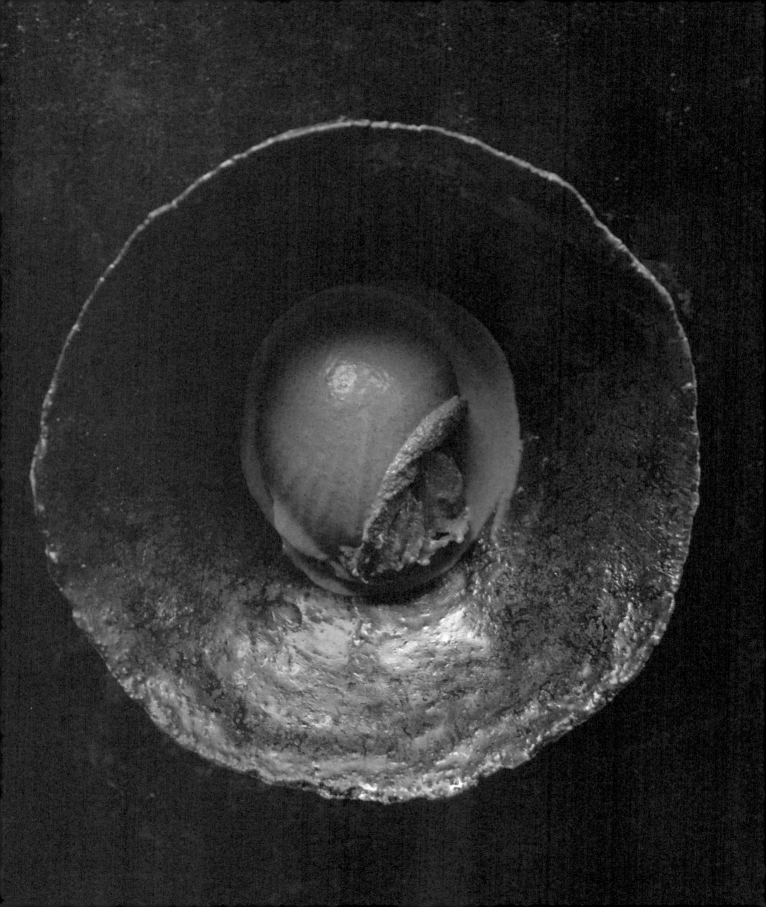

bitter nib shortbread

makes eight pieces

I have always liked shortbread, probably more than I should. It's rough but tender and able to withstand treatment. Coffee, of course, goes with it best. I've worked a bit of it into the dough, using beans for bitterness—to balance out how rich it would otherwise be. Choose your chocolate well here too. You don't want it to be so strong that it rivals the coffee.

Preheat the oven to 325°F (160°C). Set a 9-inch (23-cm) fluted tart tin with a removable base onto a baking sheet.

Put the coffee beans into a small processor or grinder and blitz to form a rough niblike texture. It doesn't have to be perfect. Set aside until needed.

In the bowl of a stand mixer fitted with the paddle attachment, beat the butter, sugar, vanilla, and salt on medium speed until pale and creamy, 3 minutes. Pause mixing to scrape down the bottom and side of the bowl. Set the speed to low and tip in the flour. Beat until it has just begun to come together, then beat in the chocolate and beans until well distributed. Tip the dough into the tin, using your fingers to press it into an even layer, then sprinkle with a pinch of gray salt.

Bake for 25 to 30 minutes, until light golden brown. Immediately use a sharp knife to score the top into eight even wedges. Allow the shortbread to cool in the tin completely before lifting out, snapping it along the scoring into pieces, and serving.

3 TABLESPOONS ROASTED COFFEE BEANS

1 CUP (2 STICKS; 230 G) UNSALTED BUTTER, *SOFTENED AT ROOM TEMPERATURE*

⅔ CUP (135 G) GRANULATED SUGAR, *PLUS A LITTLE MORE FOR THE TOP*

1 TEASPOON VANILLA EXTRACT

½ TEASPOON SALT

2 CUPS (250 G) ALL-PURPOSE FLOUR

⅔ CUP (115 G) COARSELY CHOPPED DARK CHOCOLATE

VANILLA BEAN GRAY SALT (*SEE PAGE 229*), *FOR FINISHING*

scorched cheesecake

makes a 9-inch (23-cm) cake, which serves eight to twelve

This is like a traditional Basque cheesecake. It's soft and vulnerable, but harsh, with a thin, scorched top crust. You'll want to let it darken, as the deeper it gets, the more intense it will be. I like to serve it at room temperature, enfolded in paper. It's primal, but it'd also be fine sliced up elegantly.

Preheat the oven to 400°F (200°C). Grease and line a 9-inch (23-cm) round cake pan with a depth of about 3 inches (7 cm) with two layers of parchment paper, fitting them in so that they overlap and pleat up the sides of the pan.

Put the cream cheese into the bowl of a stand mixer fitted with the paddle attachment. Beat on medium speed until smooth and malleable. Add the sugar and beat until creamy, about 3 minutes. Pause mixing to scrape down the bottom and side of the bowl. Add the eggs, one at a time, beating well to incorporate each addition, then beat in the vanilla and lemon zest. Turn the mixer speed to low. Stream in the cream and beat until just incorporated, no more than 30 seconds, then remove the bowl from the mixer and sift the flour over it. Again, resume beating, until smooth and thin. Pour into the prepared pan.

Bake for about an hour, until the edges are set and the top has developed a deep mahogany hue. It should have a fair quiver to it too. Let cool in the pan completely. It will fall with time; let it.

Once cool, use the excess parchment to carefully lift the cake out and onto a plate, peeling the paper off, if you wish. I like serving it in it, though. It's best eaten at room temperature on the day of making but will keep covered in the refrigerator for up to 3 days.

VEGETABLE OIL, *FOR GREASING THE PAN*

4 (8-OUNCE | 900 G) PACKAGES CREAM CHEESE, *AT ROOM TEMPERATURE*

1⅔ CUPS (335 G) GRANULATED SUGAR

6 LARGE EGGS

1 TEASPOON VANILLA EXTRACT

ZEST OF A LEMON

1¾ CUPS + 2 TABLESPOONS (450 ML) HEAVY CREAM

¼ CUP (30 G) ALL-PURPOSE FLOUR

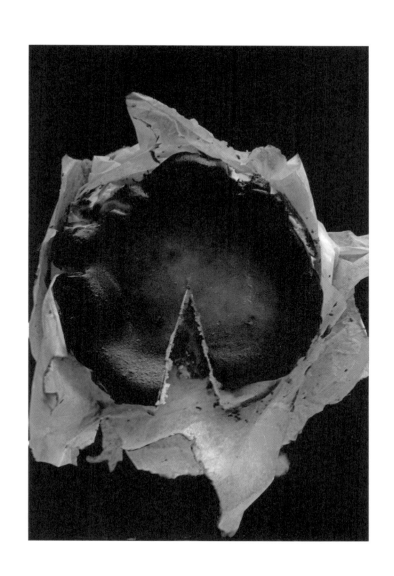

coffee parfait

serves eight

I spent the winter in Paris once, and this was something I discovered on that trip. It's hard to find parfait, least of all one that's not too sweet, icy, or dense, and a slice on Christmas Eve, shared among three people, still feels like the most precious dream. This one is my ideal. It has a texture that's part ice cream and part mousse, strong, with a deep coffee taste. It's divine but fast melting, so get in quick.

Line an 8 x 4 x 3-inch (21 x 11 x 7-cm) loaf pan with two layers of plastic wrap, leaving a slight overhang on both sides.

Put the coffee beans into a small processor or grinder and blitz to form a fine niblike texture. Tip into the base of the pan, spreading them into an even layer.

Next, in the bowl of a stand mixer fitted with the whisk attachment, whisk the cream, liqueur, vanilla, and salt until soft peaks have formed, being careful not to overwhip. You want it supple enough to fold without too much resistance. Set in the refrigerator to chill until needed.

Next, put the water, sugar, and coffee powder into a large saucepan set over medium-low heat. Heat, until the syrup reaches thread stage, 230°F (110°C), on a candy thermometer. It'll bubble heavily as it nears done, so watch it carefully.

Meanwhile, start whisking the yolks in another bowl of a stand mixer on medium speed until pale. As soon as the syrup is done, remove it from the heat and stream it into the yolks slowly, while whisking constantly. Turn the speed to high. Continue to whisk until the bowl is no longer hot to the touch, about 6 minutes. The mixture should be a caramel-ish coffee color, with a slick shine, and leave a trail when the whisk is raised.

Use a large rubber spatula to fold in thirds of the cream, each time, until just incorporated. Don't overfold. You want the parfait to retain as much air as possible, so use a gentle touch. Scrape into the prepared pan then cover and freeze until firm before serving.

2 TABLESPOONS COFFEE BEANS

1⅔ CUPS (400 ML) HEAVY CREAM

2 TABLESPOONS COFFEE LIQUEUR

1 TEASPOON VANILLA EXTRACT

A PINCH OF SALT

¾ CUP (180 ML) WATER

¾ CUP + 2 TABLESPOONS (175 G) GRANULATED SUGAR

2 TABLESPOONS COFFEE POWDER

5 LARGE EGG YOLKS

molasses gingersnap cookies

makes about fifteen cookies

Chewy, dense, and crisp, with a smoky undertone from a hit of molasses, these are addictive.

Whisk together the flour, ginger, cinnamon, allspice, nutmeg, cardamom, cloves, baking soda, and salt.

In the bowl of a stand mixer fitted with the paddle attachment, beat the butter and granulated and brown sugars on medium speed until pale caramel in color, about 3 minutes. Beat in the egg, followed by the molasses, until well combined. Lower the mixer speed and tip in the dry ingredients. Beat until a soft dough has just begun to form. Cover and transfer to the refrigerator to chill until firm, at least 30 minutes.

Meanwhile, set oven racks in the lower and upper thirds of the oven. Preheat to 350°F (180°C). Line two large baking sheets with parchment paper. Put the raw sugar in a shallow bowl.

Using a scoop or tablespoon as a measure, portion out evenly sized amounts of the dough. If you're using a spoon, use your hands to roll them into balls. Toss in the sugar until coated, then divide between the prepared sheets, placing them a few inches apart to allow for spreading.

Bake for 12 to 14 minutes, rotating the sheets top to bottom and bottom to top halfway through, until crackled. Let the cookies stand on the sheet for a few minutes before transferring them onto a wire rack to cool completely. They can be kept in an airtight container at room temperature for up to 5 days. They'll soften as they stand, though, so best get to them quick.

2 CUPS (250 G) ALL-PURPOSE FLOUR

2½ TEASPOONS GROUND GINGER

1 TEASPOON GROUND CINNAMON

½ TEASPOON GROUND ALLSPICE

¼ TEASPOON GROUND NUTMEG

¼ TEASPOON GROUND CARDAMOM

A PINCH OF GROUND CLOVES

1½ TEASPOONS BAKING SODA

½ TEASPOON SALT

½ CUP + 1 TABLESPOON (1 STICK + 1 TABLESPOON; 130 G) UNSALTED BUTTER, *SOFTENED AT ROOM TEMPERATURE*

⅓ CUP + 1 TABLESPOON (80 G) GRANULATED SUGAR

⅓ CUP (75 G) DARK BROWN SUGAR

1 LARGE EGG

¼ CUP (85 G) MOLASSES

RAW SUGAR, *FOR SANDING*

teurgoule

serves two to four

The name of this translates to "twisted mouth," and it couldn't be truer. It's a rice pudding that's done slow, creating a condensed milk–like inside and a burnt crust. You'll need to use the right dish for it. I like an earthenware pudding bowl, one that's deep, as the longer it takes, the better it gets. Shut the windows as it cooks, too, as the aroma is otherworldly.

Set an oven rack in the lower third of the oven then set a large baking sheet beneath it, to catch any excess overrun. Preheat to 300°F (150 °C).

Pour the milk into a deep saucepan. Use a sharp knife to split open the vanilla bean pod, then scrape out the seeds, adding them into the pan along with the pod and cinnamon stick. Bring to a simmer then turn off the heat and set aside to steep for 15 minutes.

Next, tumble the rice into the base of a deep earthenware pot that's about 6 inches (15 cm) deep. Pour in the milk, discarding the vanilla pod and cinnamon stick. Add the sugar and rum, then give it all a good stir to combine.

Bake for about 2 hours, until a puffed, burnished crust has formed. The time it takes will depend on the size of the dish used, so please use it as a rough guide. No two are ever alike, and that's all part of the fun. The milk should bubble and burst through as it nears done, and the inside will be thick and creamy, and the milk absorbed. Serve soon after, hot.

5 CUPS (1200 ML) WHOLE MILK

1 VANILLA BEAN POD

1 CINNAMON STICK

⅓ CUP + 1 TEASPOON (80 G) ABORIO RICE

½ CUP + 1 TABLESPOON (115 G) GRANULATED SUGAR

A SPLASH OF RUM

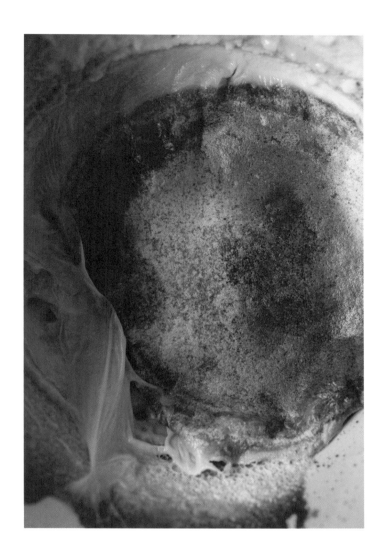

winter citrus cake

makes a 9-inch (23-cm) cake, which serves eight to twelve

There isn't much to this, save for some citrus, but that's what makes it great, especially in winter. It's bright, snowy, and comforting. You could use other types of citrus in it, like bergamot or clementine, but lemon and orange, I think, are a good standard.

Preheat the oven to 350°F (180°C). Grease and line a 9-inch (23-cm) cake pan with parchment paper.

Whisk together the ground almonds, flour, baking powder, and salt.

In the bowl of a stand mixer fitted with the paddle attachment, cream the butter and sugar on medium speed until pale and fluffy, 3 to 5 minutes. Pause mixing to scrape down the bottom and side of the bowl. Add the eggs, one at a time, beating well to incorporate each addition, then beat in the lemon and orange zests. Lower the speed. Tip in the dry ingredients and beat until well combined, then fold in the candied peel. Scrape the batter into the prepared pan.

Bake for 45 to 50 minutes, until golden brown. A skewer inserted into the middle will come out clean. Let the cake cool in the pan for 15 minutes before transferring it onto a wire rack to cool completely. Dust with confectioners' sugar before serving.

¾ CUP + 2 TABLESPOONS (1½ STICKS + 2 TABLESPOONS; 200 G) UNSALTED BUTTER, *SOFTENED AT ROOM TEMPERATURE, PLUS EXTRA FOR GREASING THE PAN*

1⅓ CUPS + 1 TEASPOON (130 G) GROUND ALMONDS

1 CUP (125 G) ALL-PURPOSE FLOUR

2 TEASPOONS BAKING POWDER

¼ TEASPOON SALT

1 CUP (200 G) GRANULATED SUGAR

3 LARGE EGGS

ZEST OF 2 LEMONS

ZEST OF AN ORANGE

½ CUP (80 G) CANDIED CITRUS PEEL

CONFECTIONERS' SUGAR, *FOR FINISHING*

BASICS

This chapter contains recipes that form the backbone of many
throughout this book. Use it as a foundation.

almond paste

makes about 1¾ cups (460 g)

I use almond paste a lot, and it's one of those things that I think is better off made at home than bought, as the kinds in stores are often too sweet, artificial in taste, or scant in pure almonds. It's not hard to make and great to always have on hand.

Put the almonds and sugar into a food processor and pulse to combine. Add in the egg white, honey, and almond extract. Process until a soft and sticky dough has begun to form around the blade. It shouldn't be too smooth but a bit clumplike, having just come together.

Scrape onto a piece of plastic wrap, then divide it in half, and shape each into a log. Chill until firm before use, about an hour. It'll keep in the refrigerator for about a week.

2½ CUPS (240 G) GROUND ALMONDS

1½ CUPS (180 G) CONFECTIONERS' SUGAR

1 LARGE EGG WHITE

1 TABLESPOON HONEY

1 TEASPOON ALMOND EXTRACT

brioche

makes two 9 x 5-inch (23 x 13-cm) loaves or about
one 2¼-pound (1 kg) batch of dough

I have a deep love for brioche; it's where it all started. I like mine with lots
of butter and egg, which results in a bread that's soft, golden, aerated, and
very, very, rich.

Heat the milk in a small saucepan until it is lukewarm in temperature. Pour
it into the bowl of a stand mixer fitted with the dough hook attachment,
then add the flour, sugar, yeast, salt, and eggs. Mix on low speed until rough
but combined, then turn the speed to medium. Knead for about another
4 minutes, until it is smooth and beginning to catch and pull around the
side of the bowl.

Add in the butter, a tablespoon at a time and waiting until it has all
incorporated before adding in another, until it is used up. Continue to
knead for about another 6 minutes, until it has developed a very velvet-like
character. Scrape into a lightly greased bowl, then cover, and leave to rise in
a warm place until doubled in size, 2 hours.

Once the dough has risen, knock it back to deflate, then re-cover and
transfer to the refrigerator to chill for at least 6 hours, but preferably
overnight. Use as directed or bake it off into loaves.

If you're planning to make loaves, line two 9 x 5 x 3-inch (23 x 13 x 7-cm)
loaf pans with parchment paper, leaving a slight overhang on both sides.

Tip the dough out and onto a floured work surface. Cut it into four equal
sized portions, then shape each into a taut ball. Divide between the prepared
pans, placing two balls in each, and placing them a few inches apart, for
rising. Cover and leave to rise until just under doubled in size, about an hour.

Meanwhile, preheat the oven to 350°F (180°C). Brush the tops of the
loaves with a thin coat of egg wash.

Bake for 30 minutes, until golden brown. Let the loaves cool in the pan for
15 minutes before lifting them out and onto a wire rack to cool further. Keep
stored in an airtight container at room temperature for up to 3 days. If they
become stale, don't fret, leftovers are great for bostock (*see page 148*).

⅓ CUP + 4 TEASPOONS (100 ML)
WHOLE MILK

4⅓ CUPS + 1 TABLESPOON
(550 G) ALL-PURPOSE FLOUR,
*PLUS MORE FOR THE WORK
SURFACE*

⅓ CUP (70 G) GRANULATED
SUGAR

4¼ TEASPOONS (14 G) INSTANT
DRIED YEAST

2 TEASPOONS SALT

6 LARGE EGGS

1 CUP (2 STICKS; 230 G)
UNSALTED BUTTER, *SOFTENED
AT ROOM TEMPERATURE*

1 LARGE EGG, *LIGHTLY BEATEN
FOR THE EGG WASH*

chantilly crème

makes 1 cup (240 ml)

This is ideal for serving alongside a lot of desserts. I flavor it with vanilla, but you could use a little almond, rose, mint, or orange blossom extract, even liqueur, instead.

In the bowl of a stand mixer fitted with the whisk attachment, whisk the cream, sugar, and vanilla seeds until soft but stable peaks have formed. Use soon after or keep cold, until needed.

1 CUP (240 ML) HEAVY CREAM

2 TABLESPOONS CONFECTIONERS' SUGAR

SEEDS OF A VANILLA BEAN POD

crème fraîche

makes about 2½ cups (360 ml)

A good crème fraîche can be hard to find. Making it at home is simple and yields the most velvety, nutty, and rich sour cream imaginable.

Pour the cream and buttermilk into a large bowl. Give it a good stir to combine, then sheathe the top with muslin or a clean kitchen towel. Let it sit, undisturbed, in a cool place and out of direct sunlight for about a day, until thick. It'll have a soured but pleasant taste when it's done. Seal and store in the refrigerator for use within a week.

2 CUPS (480 ML) HEAVY CREAM

²/₃ CUP (160 ML) CULTURED BUTTERMILK

streusel

makes about 1½ cups .

I often make a double batch of this, storing it in the freezer until needed.

Combine the flour, sugar, and salt in a medium bowl. Toss in the butter cubes. With your fingers, begin to rub the butter into the dry ingredients until large, damp clumps have formed. Use at once or seal and store in the freezer for up to three months. It can be used from frozen.

¾ CUP + 1 TABLESPOON (100 G) ALL-PURPOSE FLOUR

2 TABLESPOONS GRANULATED SUGAR

A PINCH OF SALT

¼ CUP + 2 TEASPOONS (½ STICK + 2 TEASPOONS; 70 G) UNSALTED BUTTER, *COLD AND CUT INTO ½-INCH (12-MM) CUBES*

crystallized nuts

makes about 2 cups

I like these for decorating cakes or eaten as is. They're addictive, and make great gifts too.

Preheat the oven to 350°F (180°C). Line a baking sheet with parchment paper. Scatter the nuts onto it and roast until brown, 10 to 12 minutes. Set aside to cool.

Next, put the sugar and water in a large saucepan set over medium-low heat. Heat, stirring often, until the sugar has dissolved. Turn the heat to medium and continue to cook, swirling often but not stirring, until signs of caramelization have begun to appear around the edges of the pan, about 300°F (150°C) on a candy thermometer. Remove from the heat and tip in the nuts and cinnamon.

Working quickly, stir rapidly with a wooden spoon until the syrup has hardened into a crystallized coating around the nuts. The faster you stir, the faster it'll set, and you'll need a bit of elbow grease for it at the end. Tip back onto the sheet and let cool before use.

1⅔ CUPS (220 G) CHOPPED MIXED NUTS (*HAZELNUTS, WALNUTS, PECANS, ALMONDS, CASHEWS*)

⅔ CUP + 1 TEASPOON (140 G) GRANULATED SUGAR

2 TABLESPOONS WATER

A PINCH OF GROUND CINNAMON

frangipane

makes enough to fill a 9-inch (23-cm) tart

You'll know this from a lot of pastries. It's versatile, often made with almonds, but also sometimes with hazelnuts or pistachios. I like to use it to fill tarts, which I think show it best.

In the bowl of a stand mixer fitted with the paddle attachment, beat the butter and sugar on medium speed until creamy, 3 minutes. Add in the ground almonds and beat until combined, then beat in the eggs, until incorporated. Beat in the vanilla and salt. Lower the mixer speed and tip in the flour. Turn the speed to medium-high and continue to beat until a light and aerated cream has formed. Use soon after making.

½ CUP + 2 TEASPOONS
(1 STICK + 2 TEASPOONS;
125 G) UNSALTED BUTTER,
*SOFTENED AT ROOM
TEMPERATURE*

½ CUP + 2 TABLESPOONS (125 G)
GRANULATED SUGAR

1⅔ CUPS + 1 TABLESPOON (165 G)
GROUND ALMONDS

2 LARGE EGGS

1 TEASPOON VANILLA EXTRACT

A PINCH OF SALT

¼ CUP + 1 TEASPOON (35 G)
ALL-PURPOSE FLOUR

dreamy lemon curd

makes about 2 cups (480 ml)

There's nothing about this that isn't dreamy. It's luscious, like velvet, with a bright, piquant taste. It's delicious served with almost everything, or devoured as is, with a spoon.

Put the sugar into a large heatproof bowl. Add in the zest, using your fingers to rub the ingredients together until damp and fragrant. Whisk in the eggs, egg yolks, and lemon juice.

Set the bowl over a saucepan filled with a few inches of barely simmering water set on medium-low heat. Do not allow the base of the bowl to touch the water below. Heat, whisking constantly, until the mixture is thick enough to coat the back of a spoon, about 10 minutes. It should be at a temperature of 170°F (75°C) on a candy thermometer. Remove the bowl from the saucepan.

Whisk in the butter, a tablespoon at a time, until smooth. The residual heat will be enough to melt it down. Transfer to a blender and blend on high speed for a few minutes until light and aerated. Pour into a container and cover the surface with plastic wrap to prevent a skin from forming. Transfer to the refrigerator to chill until cold, before use. It'll keep well for about a week.

1 CUP (200 G) GRANULATED
SUGAR

ZEST OF 3 LEMONS

3 LARGE EGGS

2 LARGE EGG YOLKS

¾ CUP (180 ML) LEMON JUICE

1 CUP + 2 TABLESPOONS
(2 STICKS + 2 TABLESPOONS;
255 G) UNSALTED BUTTER,
*SOFTENED AT ROOM
TEMPERATURE*

herbes de provence

makes about ¼ cup

This is a blend of herbs used mostly for savory, but also for sweet. You can purchase it, but I like to make it myself. It has a taste that reminds me of summer in France, all heat, scent, and stillness.

Mix all the ingredients together in a small bowl. Seal in a jar then store in a cool and dark place for use within the year.

2 TABLESPOONS DRIED THYME

1 TABLESPOON DRIED SUMMER SAVORY

2 TEASPOONS DRIED LAVENDER

2 TEASPOONS CHOPPED FRESH ROSEMARY LEAVES

1 TEASPOON DRIED TARRAGON

½ TEASPOON DRIED MARJORAM

½ TEASPOON GROUND ORANGE PEEL, *OPTIONAL*

¼ TEASPOON DRIED BASIL

A PINCH OF GROUND NUTMEG

pastry crust

makes enough for a 9-inch (23-cm) tart

Use this as a base for the tarts throughout these pages. I prefer to make it by hand, which I think makes for a flakier crust, but you could make it in a food processor too.

Put the flour, sugar, and salt into a large bowl. Toss in the butter, then, with your fingers, begin to rub it into the dry ingredients until the mixture resembles a coarse pebble-like meal. A few large, stray, coarser chunks of butter are fine, if not ideal, to remain. Add in the yolk, mixing it in with a wooden spoon, until combined, then add in the water. Continue to mix, being careful not to overwork it, until the dough has just started to clump together.

Tip onto a sheet of plastic wrap, using your hands to bring it together into a disc. Wrap and chill for at least an hour before use. It can be made ahead of time and kept in the refrigerator for up to 3 days, or frozen, for up to a month.

1⅓ CUPS + 1 TABLESPOON (175 G) ALL-PURPOSE FLOUR

⅓ CUP + 1 TABLESPOON (50 G) CONFECTIONERS' SUGAR

¼ TEASPOON SALT

½ CUP (1 STICK; 115 G) UNSALTED BUTTER, *COLD AND CUT INTO ½-INCH (12-MM) CUBES*

1 LARGE EGG YOLK

2 TABLESPOONS ICE WATER

rose ras el hanout

makes about ¼ cup

This Middle Eastern mélange of spices is personal. The ingredients differ according to the maker, and no two blends are ever alike. I use rose in mine, which adds a soft and sensual touch, but you could play around with it on whim. It welcomes experimentation.

Mix all the ingredients together in a small jar. Seal, then let it sit overnight, so that the aromatics have time to get to know each other, before use. Store in a cool and dark place out of direct sunlight. It will keep for a few months.

2 TABLESPOONS GROUND CINNAMON

1 TABLESPOON GROUND GINGER

3 TEASPOONS GROUND PAPRIKA

2 TEASPOONS GROUND CARDAMOM

1 TEASPOON GROUND CAYENNE

1 TEASPOON DRIED FENNEL SEEDS

1 TEASPOON GROUND NUTMEG

½ TEASPOON CRACKED BLACK PEPPER

½ TEASPOON GROUND CORIANDER

¼ TEASPOON GROUND TURMERIC

¼ TEASPOON GROUND CLOVES

¼ TEASPOON GROUND CUMIN

2 TABLESPOONS ROSE PETALS

A PINCH OF SAFFRON THREADS

vanilla bean gray salt

makes 1 cup

This is a wet salt with a taste of the sea. I infuse it with vanilla, which gives it this complex, heightened tone. It gets better the longer it sits, so make it ahead and let it mingle.

Put the salt in a medium bowl. Use a sharp knife to split open the vanilla bean pod then scrape out the seeds, stirring them into the salt. Chop the pod into small chunks then toss it in too, until distributed. Seal and leave to infuse overnight, before use. It'll keep for about six months.

1 CUP (190 G) GRAY SALT

1 VANILLA BEAN POD

index

A
After Dinner Mint Pavé 44
alcohol 13
almond paste 13
Almond Paste 223
Almond Paste Cakes 98
Amaretti 24
appliances 16
    blender 16
    coffee grinder 16
    food processor 16
    ice cream machine 16
    stand mixer 16
Atwood, Margaret 21

B
baking sheets 17
bars, Lemon Thyme Bars 33
basics 222–229
    Almond Paste 223
    Brioche 224
    Chantilly Crème 225
    Crème Fraîche 225
    Crystallized Nuts 226
    Dreamy Lemon Curd 227
    Frangipane 227
    Herbs de Provence 228
    Pastry Crust 228
    Rose Ras El Hanout 229
    Streusel 226
    Vanilla Bean Gray Salt 229
Basil Chocolate Sandwich Cookies 43
Basil Sugar Pound Cakes 36
Bay Leaf Blondies 182
Beetroot Mud Cake 162
before you begin 12–17
    equipment 15–17
    ingredients 13–15

    intention 13
    intuition 13
    mise en place 13
    mistakes 13
    reading the recipe 13
berries. *see* Bramble
biscuit cutter 16
biscuits, Oat Biscuits with Apricot,
    Rosemary, and White Chocolate
    151
Bitter Nib Shortbread 211
Blackcurrant Opera Cake 95–96
Black Forest Cookies 139
Black Tahini Brittle Ice Cream 208
blender 16
blondies
    Bay Leaf Blondies 182
    Raspberry Blondies 107
Blueberry Almond Scones 104
Bostock 148
Boysenberry Frozen Yogurt 108
Bramble 88–121
    Almond Paste Cakes 98
    Blackcurrant Opera Cake 95–96
    Blueberry Almond Scones 104
    Boysenberry Frozen Yogurt 108
    Chocolate Cassis Ice Cream 101
    Clafoutis 110
    Cocoa Brownies 114
    Currants and Cream 111
    Frangipane Tart 113
    Ganache Thumbprints 92
    Marquise 117
    Raspberry Blondies 107
    Strawberry Sumac Buckle 120
    Tayberry Granita 118
breads and pastries
    Blueberry Almond Scones 104

    Bostock 148
    Brioche 224
    Cinnamon Buns 173
    Frangipane 227
    Frangipane Tart 113
    Lavender Scones 59
    Oat Biscuits with Apricot, Rosemary,
        and White Chocolate 151
    Pastry Crust 228
    Pecan Scones 165
    Rye Bark 178
    Streusel 226
    Sugared Sesame Banana Bread
        168
Brioche 224
brownies
    Cocoa Brownies 114
    Drunken Fig Brownies 145
    Smoked Fleur de sel Brownies 192
Brown Sugar Cheesecake 174
Brutti Ma Buoni 179
buckwheat
    Buckwheat Chocolate Chunk Cookies
        176
    Malt and Buckwheat Ice Cream
        171
Burnt Sugar Ice Cream 198
butter 13

C
cake pans 17
cakes
    Almond Paste Cakes 98
    Basil Sugar Pound Cakes 36
    Beetroot Mud Cake 162
    Blackcurrant Opera Cake 95–96
    Dense Fernet Cake 46
    Double Crumb Halvah Cake 180

Espresso Marble Cake 200
Fallen Chocolate Cake 186
Fennel Pollen Pistachio Cake 30
Frosted Chamomile Tea Cake 74
Herbs de Provence Loaf 39
Late Summer Cake 126
Lemon Curd Streusel Cake 28
Parsnip Cake with Tahini Frosting 185
Rose Macaroon Cake 87
White Peach and Ginger Cake 154
White Rose Cake 76–77
Winter Citrus Cake 220
candy thermometer 16
Cantucci 34
caramel, Orange Blossom Crème Caramel 81
chamomile
    Chamomile Shortbread 82
    Frosted Chamomile Tea Cake 74
Chantilly Crème 225
cheesecake
    Brown Sugar Cheesecake 174
    Lemon Meringue Cheesecake 40–41
    Scorched Cheesecake 212
chocolate 13–14
    Basil Chocolate Sandwich Cookies 43
    Beetroot Mud Cake 162
    Buckwheat Chocolate Chunk Cookies 176
    Chocolate Cassis Ice Cream 101
    Dark Chocolate Cremeux 137
    Fallen Chocolate Cake 186
    Mendiants 73
    Rose Walnut Chocolate Chip Cookies 79
    Rye Bark 178
    Rye Chocolate Sablés 204
    S'mores Pie 203
    Truffles 160
Cinnamon Buns 173
Cixous, Héléne 189

Clafoutis 110
Cocoa Brownies 114
cocoa powder 14
coffee 14
coffee grinder 16
Coffee Parfait 215
cookies
    Basil Chocolate Sandwich Cookies 43
    Black Forest Cookies 139
    Brutti Ma Buoni 179
    Buckwheat Chocolate Chunk Cookies 176
    Ganache Thumbprints 92
    Molasses Gingersnap Cookies 217
    Rose Walnut Chocolate Chip Cookies 79
cookie scoop 16
cream
    Chantilly Crème 225
    Crème Fraîche 225
    Currants and Cream 111
    Orange Blossom Crème Caramel 81
cream cheese 14
Crème de Menthe Ice Cream 49
crème fraîche 14
Crème Fraîche 225
crumble, Red Fruit Crumble 132
Crystallized Nuts 226
cupcakes, Sea Salt Violet Cupcakes 70
Currants and Cream 111

D
Dacquoise 134
dairy ingredients 14
Dark Chocolate Cremeux 137
Dense Fernet Cake 46
digital scale 15
digital thermometer 16
Double Crumb Halvah Cake 180
Dreamy Lemon Curd 227
Drunken Fig Brownies 145
Duras, Marguerite 89

E
eggs 14
Elderflower Sabayon 65
equipment 15–17
    appliances 16
    measuring 15–16
    pans, molds, and sheets 17
    small tools 16–17
    temperature 16
espresso 14
Espresso Marble Cake 200
Evergreen 20–51
    After Dinner Mint Pavé 44
    Amaretti 24
    Basil Chocolate Sandwich Cookies 43
    Basil Sugar Pound Cakes 36
    Cantucci 34
    Crème de Menthe Ice Cream 49
    Dense Fernet Cake 46
    Fennel Pollen Pistachio Cake 30
    Herbs de Provence Loaf 39
    Juniper and White Chocolate Ice Cream 27
    Lemon Curd Streusel Cake 28
    Lemon Meringue Cheesecake 40–41
    Lemon Thyme Bars 33
    Mint Merveilleux 50

F
Fallen Chocolate Cake 186
Fennel Pollen Pistachio Cake 30
fernet, Dense Fernet Cake 46
Fig Clove Fregolotta 140
fine-mesh sieve 16
Flora 52–87
    Chamomile Shortbread 82
    Elderflower Sabayon 65
    Frosted Chamomile Tea Cake 74
    Lavender Scones 59
    Mendiants 73
    Orange Blossom Crème Caramel 81
    Petal Granola 56

Rhubarb and Pink Peppercorn Tart 66
Rose Macaroon Cake 87
Rose Walnut Chocolate Chip Cookies 79
Sea Salt Violet Cupcakes 70
Triple Bean Vanilla Ice Cream 62
Violet Mousse 69
White Rose Cake 76–77
flour 14
flowers 14. *see also* Flora
  Lavender Scones 59
  Petal Granola 56
  Rose Macaroon Cake 87
  Rose Walnut Chocolate Chip Cookies 79
  Sea Salt Violet Cupcakes 70
  Violet Mousse 69
  White Rose Cake 76–77
food processor 16
Frangipane 227
Frangipane Tart 113
Frosted Chamomile Tea Cake 74
frozen yogurt, Boysenberry Frozen Yogurt 108
fruits 14. *see also* Bramble; Orchard
  Blackcurrant Opera Cake 95–96
  Boysenberry Frozen Yogurt 108
  Currants and Cream 111
  Dacquoise 134
  Dreamy Lemon Curd 227
  Drunken Fig Brownies 145
  Fig Clove Fregolotta 140
  Lemon Curd Streusel Cake 28
  Lemon Meringue Cheesecake 40–41
  Lemon Thyme Bars 33
  Oat Biscuits with Apricot, Rosemary, and White Chocolate 151
  Plum and Hazelnut Financiers 131
  Raspberry Blondies 107

Red Fruit Crumble 132
Strawberry Sumac Buckle 120
Sugared Sesame Banana Bread 168
Tart Cherry Semifreddo 146
Tayberry Granita 118
White Peach and Ginger Cake 154

G
Ganache Thumbprints 92
grains 15
granola, Petal Granola 56

H
halvah 15
herbs and spices 14–15. *see also* Evergreen; Woodland
  After Dinner Mint Pavé 44
  Basil Chocolate Sandwich Cookies 43
  Basil Sugar Pound Cakes 36
  Bay Leaf Blondies 182
  Fennel Pollen Pistachio Cake 30
  Herbs de Provence 228
  Herbs de Provence Loaf 39
  Juniper and White Chocolate Ice Cream 27
  Lemon Thyme Bars 33
  Mint Merveilleux 50
  Molasses Gingersnap Cookies 217
  Oat Biscuits with Apricot, Rosemary, and White Chocolate 151
  Rhubarb and Pink Peppercorn Tart 66
  Rose Ras El Hanout 229
  White Peach and Ginger Cake 154

I
ice cream
  Black Tahini Brittle Ice Cream 208
  Burnt Sugar Ice Cream 198
  Chocolate Cassis Ice Cream 101

Crème de Menthe Ice Cream 49
Juniper and White Chocolate Ice Cream 27
Malt and Buckwheat Ice Cream 171
Mulled Wine Ice Cream 143
Triple Bean Vanilla Ice Cream 62
ice cream machine 16
impermanence 11
ingredients 13–15
  alcohol 13
  almond paste 13
  butter 13
  chocolate 13–14
  coffee 14
  dairy ingredients 14
  eggs 14
  espresso 14
  flour 14
  flowers 14
  fruit 14
  grains 15
  halvah 15
  herbs 14–15
  leavenings 15
  nuts 15
  oil 15
  salt 15
  seeds 15
  spices 14
  sugar 15
  tahini 15
  vanilla 15
  yeast 15
intention 13
intuition 13

J
Juniper and White Chocolate Ice Cream 27

K
kitchen torch 16

L
Late Summer Cake 126
Lavender Scones 59
leavenings 15
Lemon Curd Streusel Cake 28
Lemon Meringue Cheesecake 40–41
Lemon Thyme Bars 33
Lispector, Clarice 53
loaf pans 17

M
Malt and Buckwheat Ice Cream 171
Marquise 117
mascarpone 14
measuring cups 15
measuring equipment 15–16
    digital scale 15
    measuring cups 15
    measuring spoons 16
Mendiants 73
mint
    After Dinner Mint Pavé 44
    Crème de Menthe Ice Cream 49
    Mint Merveilleux 50
mise en place 13
mistakes 13
mixing bowls 16
Molasses Gingersnap Cookies 217
molds. see pans, molds, and sheets
mousse, Violet Mousse 69
Mulled Wine Ice Cream 143

N
natural narrative 11
nuts 15
    Almond Paste 223
    Amaretti 24
    Blueberry Almond Scones 104

Crystallized Nuts 226
Fennel Pollen Pistachio Cake 30
Pecan Scones 165
Plum and Hazelnut Financiers 131
Rose Walnut Chocolate Chip Cookies 79

O
Oat Biscuits with Apricot, Rosemary, and White Chocolate 151
oil 15
Oliver, Mary 11
Orange Blossom Crème Caramel 81
Orchard 122–155
    Black Forest Cookies 139
    Bostock 148
    Dacquoise 134
    Dark Chocolate Cremeux 137
    Drunken Fig Brownies 145
    Fig Clove Fregolotta 140
    Late Summer Cake 126
    Mulled Wine Ice Cream 143
    Oat Biscuits with Apricot, Rosemary, and White Chocolate 151
    Pêche De Vigne Sorbet 128
    Plum and Hazelnut Financiers 131
    Red Fruit Crumble 132
    Tart Cherry Semifreddo 146
    White Peach and Ginger Cake 154
oven thermometer 16

P
pans, molds, and sheets 17
    baking sheets 17
    cake pans 17
    loaf pans 17
    pie dishes 17
    specialty molds 17
    tart pan 17
Parsnip Cake with Tahini Frosting 185
Pastry Crust 228

Pecan Scones 165
Pêche De Vigne Sorbet 128
Petal Granola 56
pie dishes 17
Plum and Hazelnut Financiers 131

R
Raspberry Blondies 107
recipe, reading through 13
Red Fruit Crumble 132
Rhubarb and Pink Peppercorn Tart 66
rolling pin 17
Rose Macaroon Cake 87
Rose Ras El Hanout 229
Rose Walnut Chocolate Chip Cookies 79
Rye Bark 178
Rye Chocolate Sablés 204

S
salt 15
salt types 15
scones
    Blueberry Almond Scones 104
    Lavender Scones 59
    Pecan Scones 165
Scorched Cheesecake 212
Sea Salt Violet Cupcakes 70
seeds 15
Sexton, Anne 157
sheets. see pans, molds, and sheets
shortbread, Chamomile Shortbread 82
small tools. see tools, small
small utensils 17
Smoke 188–221
    Bitter Nib Shortbread 211
    Black Tahini Brittle Ice Cream 208
    Burnt Sugar Ice Cream 198
    Coffee Parfait 215
    Espresso Marble Cake 200
    Molasses Gingersnap Cookies 217
    Rye Chocolate Sablés 204

Scorched Cheesecake 212

Smoked Fleur de sel Brownies 192

S'mores Pie 203

Teurgoule 218

Tiramisu 194

Walnut Snowballs 197

Winter Citrus Cake 220

Smoked Fleur de sel Brownies 192

S'mores Pie 203

sorbet, Pêche De Vigne Sorbet 128

specialty molds 17

spices 14. *see also* herbs and spices

stand mixer 16

staples. *see* ingredients

Streusel 226

sugar 15

Sugared Sesame Banana Bread 168

sugar types 15

sumac, Strawberry Sumac Buckle 120

T

tahini 15

Tart Cherry Semifreddo 146

tart pan 17

tarts

Frangipane Tart 113

Rhubarb and Pink Peppercorn Tart 66

Teurgoule 218

thermometers 16

digital or candy thermometer 16

oven thermometer 16

Tiramisu 194

tools, small 16–17

biscuit cutter 16

cookie scoop 16

fine-mesh sieve 16

kitchen torch 16

mixing bowls 16

rolling pin 17

small utensils 17

wire rack 17

Triple Bean Vanilla Ice Cream 62

Truffles 160

V

vanilla 15

Triple Bean Vanilla Ice Cream 62

Vanilla Bean Gray Salt 229

vegetables, Rhubarb and Pink Peppercorn Tart 66

W

Walnut Snowballs 197

white chocolate

Juniper and White Chocolate Ice Cream 27

Oat Biscuits with Apricot, Rosemary, and White Chocolate 151

White Peach and Ginger Cake 154

wine

Drunken Fig Brownies 145

Mulled Wine Ice Cream 143

Winter Citrus Cake 220

Winterson, Jeanette 123

wire rack 17

Woodland 156–187

Bay Leaf Blondies 182

Beetroot Mud Cake 162

Brown Sugar Cheesecake 174

Brutti Ma Buoni 179

Buckwheat Chocolate Chunk Cookies 176

Cinnamon Buns 173

Double Crumb Halvah Cake 180

Fallen Chocolate Cake 186

Malt and Buckwheat Ice Cream 171

Parsnip Cake with Tahini Frosting 185

Pecan Scones 165

Rye Bark 178

Sugared Sesame Banana Bread 168

Truffles 160

Y

yeast 15

Z

Zanotti, Fanny 174

ACKNOWLEDGMENTS

To:

Irene, Agatha, Alice, Amy, Anaïs, Andrei, Anne, Audrey, Claire, Clarice, Cristina, David, Dietmar, Hélène, Henry, Jane, Jerôme, Joe, Johnny, Leonard, Lindy, Louise, Lydia, Margaret, Marguerite, Marlon, Patti, Raymond, Roseanne, Sylvia, the team at Harper Design, Valerie, X, and You, the reader—whom I wouldn't be here without.

ABOUT THE AUTHOR

Thalia Ho is a food writer, cook, and creator of the award-winning food blog *Butter and Brioche*. Her work is known for its explorative combinations, decadence, and prose. She resides in Australia but travels the world often in search of sweetness.

HarperCollins books may be purchased for educational, business, or
sales promotional use. For information please email the Special Markets
Department at SPsales@harpercollins.com.

First published in 2021 by Harper Design
An Imprint of HarperCollins*Publishers*
195 Broadway
New York, NY 10007
Tel: (212) 207-7000
Fax: (855) 746-6023
harperdesign@harpercollins.com
www.hc.com

Page 21: Excerpted from *Power Politics*, copyright © 1971
by Margaret Atwood. Reproduced with permission from
House of Anansi Press Inc., Toronto. www.houseofanansi.com

Front-cover illustrations from *Food and Drink: A Pictorial Archive
from Nineteenth-Century Sources*, Dover Pictorial Archives (1983).

Distributed throughout the world by
HarperCollins*Publishers*
195 Broadway
New York, NY 10007

ISBN 978-0-06-295842-6
Library of Congress Control Number: 20039213

Design by Amanda Jane Jones
Photographs by Thalia Ho

Printed in Malaysia
First Printing, 2021